T0129312

The Seven Angels of Peace

Ancient Essene Wisdom
for Today's World

SARAH ANNE BARKER

BALBOA.PRESS

A DIVISION OF HAY HOUSE

Balboa Press books may be ordered through booksellers or by contacting:

Balboa Press
A Division of Hay House
1663 Liberty Drive
Bloomington, IN 47403
www.balboapress.com.au
1 (877) 407-4847

Because of the dynamic nature of the Internet, any web addresses or links contained in this book may have changed since publication and may no longer be valid. The views expressed in this work are solely those of the author and do not necessarily reflect the views of the publisher, and the publisher hereby disclaims any responsibility for them.

The author of this book does not dispense medical advice or prescribe the use of any technique as a form of treatment for physical, emotional, or medical problems without the advice of a physician, either directly or indirectly. The intent of the author is only to offer information of a general nature to help you in your quest for emotional and spiritual well-being. In the event you use any of the information in this book for yourself, which is your constitutional right, the author and the publisher assume no responsibility for your actions.

Any people depicted in stock imagery provided by Getty Images are models, and such images are being used for illustrative purposes only. Certain stock imagery © Getty Images.

Interior Image Credit: Angel illustrations by Frances Clarke

Print information available on the last page.

ISBN: 978-1-5043-1984-3 (sc)
ISBN: 978-1-5043-1983-6 (e)

Balboa Press rev. date: 12/03/2019

Contents

Acknowledgements ix

Introduction xi

Chapter 1   The Essenes 1

Chapter 2   The Angels of Peace 9

Chapter 3   The Rainbow Bridge 14

Chapter 4   Day One, Sunday Angel of Life 19

Chapter 5   Day Two, Monday Angel of Power 33

Chapter 6   Day Three, Tuesday Angel of Love 53

Chapter 7   Day Four, Wednesday Angel of Creative Work...... 63

Chapter 8   Day Five, Thursday Angel of Wisdom 75

Chapter 9   Day Six, Friday Angel of Joy 89

Chapter 10 Day Seven, Saturday Angel of Eternal Life 99

Chapter 11 The Angels Are with Us 110

Chapter 12 The Angel Peace Meditation 112

Chapter 13 Seven Angels in Seven Days 115

Bibliography 125

Notes 127

To my father

Acknowledgements

I would like to express my love and heartfelt gratitude to the following people: my partner, James, for his belief in my work and for holding a loving space within which I could write this book; my sister, Frances Clarke, who has given us the gift of the angel illustrations and whose work transmits an energy of pure light; and June Hope, my dear friend who has encouraged me through the many processes of becoming an author and who also spent many hours reading and editing my work.

My teacher and mentor, Mike Booth, principal of the Aura-Soma Academy, has guided me to follow my star within and manifest my soul purpose. The Aura-Soma colour system has been my tool for spiritual growth, enabling a connection to open within me, to the Essenes and the angels. Although I did not meet her, I feel an immense gratitude to Vicky Wall, who birthed the Aura-Soma system in 1983, a colour system for self-discovery and conscious change.

Edmond Bordeaux Szekely gave us the gift of the translations of the ancient Essene texts—a precious gift of peace for humankind, our Mother Earth, and all other sentient beings.

Ultimately my love and gratitude are to the angels, our unseen companions in all aspects of life.

Introduction

My mission as I write this book is to share the wisdom of the Essenes, as a living, breathing teaching from the heart; as an experience of nature and her angels; and as a connection with the divine feminine. The living book of nature and her angels is here for all to see. My wish is this book will open a new vista to the eyes and hearts of those who read it—one of peace, joy, and hope for new beginnings.

This book is an invitation to peace. In the words of the Essenes, "peace is that for which the world most yearns." They believed the angels were messengers of peace and that angels were conscious, sentient beings who wished to help humanity and the planet.

This book is an opportunity to bring the peace of the angels into your life—a peace that is sevenfold, embracing all aspects of our personal lives and life on the planet. This book shares the wisdom of each of the seven angels of peace and touches the essence of the Essene teachings, whose teachings were like no other. There have often been teachers of peace, but few have spoken of the angels of peace and the complete peace that is possible when we invite them into our lives.

We often ask ourselves, How can I live a more spiritual, peaceful, and meaningful life? How can I help or make a difference? My wish is to empower and enable—to show how we can each make a positive contribution to peace, for ourselves, for others, and for the planet. We can be part of the solution, creating the peace we wish to see in the world. We live in a new time, when consciousness is beginning to change upon the planet, as many people are beginning to search for answers in a new way.

The ancient teachings of the Essenes were written on papyrus scrolls and hidden in caves and vaults. Two thousand years later, they were rediscovered. The gift of translation of these precious documents was given to humanity by Edmond Bordeaux Szekely, in *The Essene Gospel of Peace*, where he has captured the poetic beauty of the words of the Essenes. The translations of the texts of the Essenes are the basis for this book.

It feels as though the words of the Essenes have been in a time capsule, waiting to be opened and released into the world. My perception is that there was a timeline, designed for them to be available again in this time, the dawning of the new earth, and a greater conscious awareness.

I wrote this book as an offering to those of us who are here on the planet now, at the beginning of the new time. I wrote this book for the mother earth, Gaia, and all of her angels so that more people may open their hearts and minds to the angels, our invisible helpers and guides. For it is with their love that we may create the peace we wish to see and be in the world.

We often personify angels, but they are beings of a vast consciousness. There are many different realms of angels, but the ones I especially share with you in this book are the angels of peace. Their energy has been strong and present as I wrote this book.

The "how-to" in relation to creating peace in our life with the angels, is the practise of the angel meditations, and these are shared as part of this book. After we have met each of the angels, we come to the practise. This is a simple daily meditation on each of the seven days of the week, while invoking one of the angels of peace. This is the gift of peace from the Essenes who practised the same meditation all those years ago, and the words quoted to invoke the angels are based on the words they used.

My belief is that the Essenes had a message of love and peace for all people, as their message transcended the boundaries of countries and cultures. As such I have chosen to modify some of the words of the translations to a more ecumenical form, to suit these modern times. Hence, I have used the name *Mother*

Earth, in place of the *Earthly Mother*, and the *Divine*, in place of the *Heavenly Father*. I have also simplified the language used for the angel invocations for our ease of use in these modern times.

As a reference to use in our practise of peace with the angels, the final chapter, "Seven Angels in Seven Days," includes the daily cycle of angel meditations in a simple format for us to refer to.

My hope is this book will bring you the peace and joy of the angels.

Chapter 1

The Essenes

A race by themselves, more remarkable than any
other in this wide world.
—Pliny, a contemporary of the Essenes

The world of angels was an everyday reality for the Essenes.
They believed the sun, the wind, the water, and the earth were
angels, and that the flowers and trees were conscious beings. The
eyes of the Essenes had been opened to a spiritual realm hidden
to most—that of the realm of the angels in nature.

The Essenes observed the world of nature with different eyes.
They saw, with an inner vision, a reality not visible to most. They
saw within nature the presence of angels.

To speak of the Essenes is to speak about nature. They believed
there to be a spiritual quality within nature and that every leaf,
drop of water, and ray of sunlight was infused with this spiritual
quality.

To the Essene, the secrets of life were encoded in nature. The
forms and shapes of nature, such as the perfection of the shell of a
snail or the whorls of a pine cone spoke to them of the secrets in
nature and of the perfect symmetry and form that are expressions
of a perfect and divine order.

They lived a life of quintessential joy, abundant with angels
and happiness. They were great gardeners and agriculturists, and
even though they lived in the desert, they created abundant and
verdant gardens because they gardened cocreatively with the
angels.

They were healers of people outside of their community and

were wise and compassionate teachers. They believed in equality and fairness for all and taught about peace and love, but they were persecuted for being different, as they lived in a time when their country had been invaded by the Romans.

Their teachings echo down the centuries and were expressed as an essence of truth, which can be found within the traditions of the gnostics, the Cathars, and the master craftsmen and women. Their teachings were instilled with the quintessence of peace and love.

They came out of ancient Egypt as part of the people of Israel led by Moses. They were the high initiates of the mystery schools and were the keepers of the ancient teachings and the secrets of the angels.

Angels were a part of their everyday life. Their whole calendar and cycle of day and night was woven around their relationship with the angels. They invoked the angels into everything they did, even their thoughts and how they were feeling. They knew the frailties of being human and had immense compassion for those who were suffering.

They lived somewhat separately from their contemporaries. They were naturally desert people but also had communal houses in the towns. These were places where those in need could go for healing, as the Essenes were highly revered for their healing skills.

The Essenes were a spiritually rarefied group of people, whose teachings have rippled through the mists of time, contained within ancient texts and prayers. They taught about right livelihood and how to take responsibility for the thoughts and feelings. They taught about angels and the path of peace. They taught about love. In the eyes of the Essenes, the angels were friends, life companions who taught them about peace and joy.

Some of the highest initiates of the Essenes were women, as to be able to commune with the angels of nature is a gift of the intuition, a faculty most easily felt by the feminine. The texts of the Essene teachings we have inherited, while often patriarchal in their tone, are essentially feminine in the practise they share.

The patriarchal teachings we have inherited describe the structure and form of their society, the rules they lived by. To delve into the secret mysteries of the Essenes is to reveal the soft pages of their inner teachings and the teachings of the angels.

The Essene initiates knew words were purely the framework upon which the intuition could flow. The intuition is the feminine, inner knowing, the connection with our inner wisdom. This is the path of the mystic, unravelling the mysteries of life and creation, and it is through the intuition we connect with the realm of the angels.

The Essenes had reached a level of spiritual development rare in human history. They believed they were part of a creative process and that their purpose was to work with the angels to create a paradise on Earth.

They believed every tree and living plant, every animal, fish, and grain of sand was part of a creation story. They saw reflections of the Divine in every drop of rain and believed all these things, even the mountains, were part of one holistic, cosmic organism that we call Earth. They considered both the visible and invisible worlds to be part of this organism, the visible world of nature and the invisible world of the angels. They lived on the earth in harmonious unity with this living, cosmic organism and with both the seen and unseen realms. They believed to live consciously and cocreatively with these realms was the rightful place and birthright of humanity.

Essene Life

The Essenes lived separately from the rest of the people of the Holy Land. They created their own communities, where the nucleus of their society was the family. They saw family life as an opportunity to demonstrate love in action, although not all Essenes lived in family units, as some chose the more solitary spiritual path. They had centres of teaching and advanced spiritual practise, high temples of the Essene tradition. Qumran was their most revered centre, overlooking the Dead Sea, the desert, and the River Jordan. And it was here, in nearby caves, that the Dead Sea scrolls were found. The ancient texts had been preserved by the Essenes in clay jars, so that we may access their library two thousand years later and learn from the wisdom of the past

Whether they lived within a family or solitarily, the Essenes aspired to live as one with nature, even eating with the cycles of the sun. They ate at noon, when the sun was high in the sky, and again after sundown. They ate in silence to honour the gift of food from the Mother Earth.

They were cocreative gardeners with the angels, producing a cornucopia of fruit, nuts, and grains in the deserts of the Middle East. They built their communities close to the rivers or lakes to connect with the angel of water. They walked barefoot on the Mother Earth, to receive her life-giving energies, and feel connected with the mother. They aspired to be examples of right livelihood and to express love in all the little things in life.

The initiated Essene was able to accomplish extraordinary things because of their spiritual and purification practises. They lived a vibrant life of up to 140 years old, functioning with abundant health and vitality. They were fruitarians, eating only what nature offered and what they had grown themselves. They ate a raw diet, food abundantly rich with life force from the Mother Earth—fruit; dried fruit and nuts; sprouted wheat; and also milk, herbs, and honey in the winter. They were very particular with their purification rituals, bathing several times each day in cold water. Both these cleansing rituals and their rarefied diet contributed to their unusual health and longevity.

To the Essenes, the highest accolades were given to those who lived alone in the desert. The initiated Essenes were so adept at living as one with nature, they were able to sustain themselves in a barren desert. They would collect the morning dew to drink and were experienced at fasting, so required little food to thrive on. The small quantity of food they ate was chewed very slowly to extract the living life force of the food. To live a singular life in the desert was the ultimate expression of living in symbiotic union with nature, the elements, and all of the angels.

The Essenes were committed to a thrice daily cycle of meditations with the angels. They meditated at dawn, noon and in the evening after sundown, as these times are windows of opportunity for ease of connection with the angels. As in their eating, the timing of their meditations followed the path of the sun. The pinnacle of their day was the peace meditation with the angels, which was practised each day at noon.

The Mystical Essene

> Be still and know I am God.
> —"The Vision of Enoch"
> in The Essene Gospel of Peace

This is the main tenet of the vision of Enoch, who the Essenes considered to be their great forefather. Enoch had lived a perfect life, invoking the angels into everything he thought, everything he felt, and everything he did. The legend says that Enoch became "divine man," who was "taken" by God and became the archangel Metatron. The Essenes aspired to emulate Enoch and live as perfect a life as possible—in their thoughts, their feelings, their relationships, and their work.

Enoch had been given the secrets of the angels. They say "the angels touched his brow" and gave him the secrets of the archangel Ratziel. Enoch became the keeper of the ancient mysteries. These secrets were passed down through the generations, to eventually settle in the heads and hearts of the people known as the Essenes.

A unique quality of the Essenes was their belief in angels. They not only believed in angels, but also invoked them into every aspect of their lives. The realm of angels was a reality to them, even though they were invisible to most.

They studied the ancient texts they had inherited from Enoch and their ancestors, as well as the living book of nature, the words of which were given to them by the Mother Earth—their aspiration being to live in unity with the Mother Earth and her angels. There have been many communities of spiritual aesthetes over the centuries, but the Essenes were unique in their belief in and cooperative relationship with angels. They considered themselves to work in cocreative partnership with the angels.

The angels are messengers and teachers, who are closer to us at this time because of the changes that are occurring on the earth. The Essenes had many different angels who they invited into their lives. Their practise was to meditate and commune with the angels, which means they believed they were communicating directly with the angels. They believed the angels were "living," sentient beings with vast, cosmic intelligence, who they could learn from them.

While angels themselves are without doctrine or dogma, there are ancient spiritual systems that may help us to understand what may seem incomprehensible—systems that help us to understand the world of the angels, and one of these is the Tree of Life. In the Judaic tradition, the Tree of Life is known as the Kabbalah, which was also known of by the Essenes, as the Judaic stream was part of their own heritage. But the Essenes had their own Tree of Life, which was the secret given by the archangel Ratziel to Enoch and passed down, through oral tradition, to the Essenes, who were the guardians of this mystical truth.

To the Essenes, nature was our greatest teacher, and the tree was a symbol of spiritual wholeness and unity. The mystical

Essene Tree of Life had seven branches and seven roots. They believed the branches of the tree were the angels of the Divine, and the roots of the tree were the angels of the Mother Earth. They believed that humankind sat at the centre of the tree, so communing with all of the angels of the Divine and all of the angels of the Mother Earth.

The angels of the Essene Tree of Life were the angels they communed with every dawn and every evening, and these were the angels of their innermost mystical path, knowledge of which was only given to those initiated into their inner circle. The angels of the roots of the Tree of Life are the angels of nature. These are the angels of the sun, water, air, earth, life, joy and the Mother Earth.

The angels of the branches of the Tree of Life are those who stretch their wingtips up towards the Divine. These are the angels of power, love, wisdom, eternal life, creative work, peace, and the Divine.

Angels were the way, the truth, and the light of Essene life. Other angels they meditated with were the seventy-two angels of creation, the angels of the seasons, and those of their holy days. They invoked the angels into everything they thought, every word they spoke, and every action they did. They believed our thoughts and feelings create invisible beings on the ethers, and they wished to create peaceful, loving, and wise beings, which is why they invoked the angels into everything they thought, said, and did. They always focused on the positive, as they knew that's what would grow. In the world of the Essenes, the angels were their spiritual friends, who taught them of peace, love, and joy.

They were messengers of peace, and they lived a life of supreme peace. They imprinted the energy field of the earth with peace wherever they went. The peace of the Essenes was no ordinary peace. It was not a transient feeling of relaxation. It was an endless peace with limitless boundaries; it was a complete peace, beyond our normal human comprehension. Their peace was one of unity and an expression of living in alignment with the One Law, as above, so below. They believed the earth, in all her beauty, was a reflection of the Divine.

They travelled widely to instil the energy of peace into the energetic grid system of the Earth—creating a healing energy of peace that is still tangible in some of the places they visited, even though it was over two thousand years ago.

The annual calendar they lived by was also an expression of their living in alignment with the laws of nature. Their new year was the first day of spring, the spring equinox, which they called the head of the year. The fresh new growth of spring was the signal for their new year, in complete alignment with the rebirth in nature.

Their annual solar calendar was given to them by archangel Uriel, an angel messenger of the sun. This was the calendar they had lived by since the time of Enoch, who some consider to have been the first Essene. Each new year and each new season always began on the fourth day of their week, which, in their creation story, was the day the sun was created.

Both their daily and their annual, cycles followed the path of the sun. Their first angel meditation of the day was at dawn, just as the sun was rising, and their final angel meditation was just after the sun had set. When the sun was high in the sky, they held their peace meditation with the angels.

Chapter 2

The Angels of Peace

Only he who is at peace with all the angels can shed the light of peace on others.
—*The Essene Gospel of Peace*

The Essenes lived a life of infinite peace. They lived the life of peace they wished to see in the world. They were teachers of peace and taught about the angels, the seven paths of peace, and the gifts the angels bring to us. This had been an Essene practise for thousands of years. It was one of their secret inner teachings, which had been reserved for the initiates of their community.

There came a time, two thousand years ago, when they began to share this teaching with those outside of their community. This was their gift of peace to humanity, a gift of peace so precious it is still relevant today.

The Essenes believed the whole of humanity was sorely in need of peace and that it was the angels who could bring the peace humanity needed. The peace of the angels surpasses any other peace possible. It is a gift of extraordinary peace—one that encompasses the whole of life.

The Essenes believed the lack of peace lay behind all discord of any kind. Whether it was poor health, family rifts, injustice, or even wars, they believed all of these things were created by a lack of peace. To the Essenes, people were not at peace within themselves, let alone with each other.

They believed, if one person was unpeaceful, that lack of peace would affect all others. Each one of us is a microcosm of thoughts and feelings, and whatever we think or feel affects the macrocosm, the greater whole. When we feel peaceful, the converse is true, for then that peace will ripple out to those near and far.

To the Essenes, peace was a practise and a quality that could grow, and their practise to create peace was to meditate with the angels. There were seven angels they meditated with, who were known as the seven angels of peace.

These angels are the angel of life, the angel of power, the angel of love, the angel of creative work, the angel of wisdom, the angel of joy, and the angel of the divine. Each of these angels of peace brings us a particular gift of peace:

- Angel of eternal life—Peace with the Divine
- Angel of joy—Peace with the Mother Earth
- Angel of wisdom—Peace with culture
- Angel of creative work—peace with humanity
- Angel of love—Peace with our family
- Angel of power—Peace with our mind
- Angel of life—Peace with our body

The peace of the angels is an all-encompassing peace, which embraces all aspects of life and living. It is a gift of peace for each person, for their family and thoughts, for those who we know and those who we don't know. It is peace with the Mother Earth and with different cultures and beliefs, and it is a peace with the Divine or what we may call God.

For the Essenes:

Many are those who do not know peace, for they are at war with their own body, they are at war with their thoughts, they have no peace with their fathers, their mothers, their children, they have no peace with their friends and neighbours, they

know not the beauty of the Holy Scrolls, they
labour not through the day in the kingdom of the
Mother Earth, nor do they sleep at night in the
arms of the Divine. (*The Essene Gospel of Peace*)

The Essenes aspired to think peaceful thoughts, feel peaceful
emotions, and be peaceful in everything they did. The dream of
the Essene was to be like an angel—to think as an angel, to speak
as an angel, and to do what an angel would do. The gifts of the
angels of peace lived in their bodies, as they personified the peace
of the angels.

Now we will begin to meet the angels who were so highly
revered by the Essenes and were a part of their daily spiritual
practise—the angels who have been waiting in the wings for
millennia, to share their gifts of peace with us.

The Angels of Power, Love, and Wisdom

The paths are seven through the Infinite Garden,
and each must be traversed by the body, the heart
and the mind as one.

—*The Essene Gospel of Peace*

The Essenes believed our essential nature is peace, and that
we each have a divine spark of peace inside us. They believed
humanity had lost touch with this peace, and they taught there
is a path we can follow where we can find this peace again. We
may think of the path to peace as seven paths through a forest,
and sometimes the way is hidden. But the seven angels of peace
are our guides through the forest. They lead us on our path to
peace, with the seven gifts of peace as our prize.

We tread this path with the whole of our being—with our
body, our heart and our mind. In addition to the seven angels of

peace, there are three angels who are always with us, whichever of the seven paths we tread. These are the angel of wisdom, the angel of love, and the angel of power.

These three angels are always by our side, as the angels ask us to travel each of the seven paths in three ways, with our thoughts, our feelings, and our bodies. Our thoughts, our feelings, and our bodies are not separate, and we need to find peace in all three.

The angel of wisdom will guide our thoughts, the angel of love will purify our feelings, and the angel of power will bring our love and wisdom together, so we may express it in our actions. We will meet the angel of peace, the angel the Essenes revered above all.

The Angel of Peace

> Of all the angels of the Divine, peace is that for which the world most yearns.
>
> —*The Essene Gospel of Peace*

The angel of peace is the angel the Essenes revered above all, and they invoked this angel as a prelude to each of the seven daily angel meditations. The Angel of Peace is an angel distinct from the seven angels of peace, and they communed with this angel every day, so as to bring its qualities of peace and love to the earth.

The angel of peace is as mysterious as the night sky and encompasses the whole of the earth in each moment. She holds the quintessence of love in her hand and gifts us with love as a balm to all that is unpeaceful.

The angel of peace is an omnipresent guide overlighting each of the seven paths of peace. The peace of this angel is beyond our understanding, as it is a divine peace. It is the peace of our dreams and the aspiration of the Essenes, a unified peace with all.

The Essenes invoked the presence of the angel of peace to

commence each of the seven meditations of peace, for the peace this angel offers is an ineffable peace unknown to most. It is the peace the great teachers spoke of.

> I will invoke peace, whose breath is friendly, and whose hand smooths the troubled brow. In the reign of peace there is neither hunger nor thirst, neither cold wind nor hot wind, neither old age nor death.
>
> —*The Essene Gospel of Peace*

Chapter 3

The Rainbow Bridge

First be at peace with all of the angels, for then
your peace will be as a fountain that replenishes
itself with the giving. And the more you give, so
the more you will be given, for such is the Law.

—*The Essene Gospel of Peace*

We are each a rainbow of light, like a droplet of rain with the
sun shining through. The colours of the rainbow are the same as
the colours of our chakras, which are a part of our body of light.
The chakras appear as wheels of light and are aligned along the
length of our spine, from the base to the crown, each having a
specific vibration of light.

We have the red of the root chakra, at the base of the spine;
the orange of the sacral chakra; the yellow of the solar plexus; the
green of the heart; the blue of the throat; the royal blue of the
brow; and the violet of the crown.

Our chakras are an intimate connection point between the
body, mind, and soul. The clarity, or lack of clarity, of our chakras
has a profound impact upon our physical, mental, emotional, and
spiritual well-being. When our chakras are colourful and clear,
our bodies function well, and our emotions and thoughts are
harmonious. If our chakras are cloudy or blocked, the body, mind,
and feelings will be out of balance.

To feel happy and healthy and to live our lives more consciously
and mindfully is to live our life in a more enlightened way. This
literally means that our body and our energy body will be more
full of light and our chakras will be clear in their rainbow colours.

Peace can only come when we are in balance—when our rainbow colours are shining brightly—as this is when the body, mind, and spirit are operating in harmony.

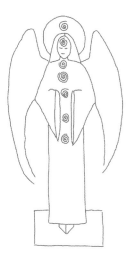

The seven chakras

We are one with the colours of nature; the hues and tints of the flowers; the rocks and crystals; and, most of all, the light of the sun. The angels say we are destined to be like the sun, with our colours shining and bright. We are one with the earth, the sun, and the rainbow; our nature is one and the same.

The rainbow is a gift from the angels and a bridge between heaven and earth. The angels help us to build our own rainbow, illuminating the colours of our chakras. The rainbow is our bridge to peace, which we can build one day at a time with the angels. There is one angel each day, one colour each day, and one gift of peace from the angels each day.

This was the ongoing cycle of daily meditations for the Essenes, which we can practise now too. They held their meditations with the angels when the sun was high in the sky, as this was when the potential for peace and healing was greatest. The seven angels, the seven gifts of peace, and the seven colours are aligned with the seven days of the week, always in a set order.

The meditation cycle creates a rainbow of peace, beginning at the root chakra on the first day of the week and completing at the crown on the seventh. We journey through the seven days of the week, with one angel, one chakra, and one gift of peace each day.

As we build our rainbow of peace with the angels, we become a chalice of light to receive their gifts. The cycle of daily meditations is ongoing. It is a commitment we can make if we wish that will bring the light of peace of the angels to our life. The meditations are an alchemical process of healing as we fill our body with light. The light will flow in and replace anything that was dark or dim or unpeaceful.

As we practise the meditations, we enter a process of personal and spiritual growth, as to invite in the angels is to create positive change. The gift we receive is the peace, which is sevenfold, a gift the angels hold dear. We become our own rainbow and our own pot of gold, so we may share our own light of peace in the world.

In the next seven chapters, we meet the seven angels of peace. The world of the angels is rich and abundant, so much more than we can normally perceive, as the angels will open our eyes to a new vista around us. The realm of peace is not somewhere else; it is here within us already. The change we wish to see happens inside us as the angels purify and enlighten our being.

Each of the following seven chapters commences with the unique words spoken by the Essenes of their invocations to the angels. Each is rich in its simplicity and pertains to the chakra of the day and the gift each angel brings.

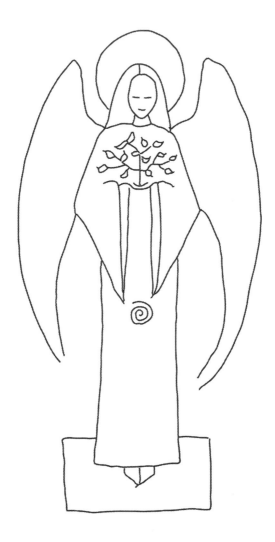

Angel of life

Chapter 4

Day One, Sunday
Angel of Life

Angel invocation

> I ask the Angel of Peace to always be with me, and I ask the Angel of Life to bring health and vitality to my body.
>
> —*The Essene Gospel of Peace*

The gift of the angel of life: Peace with our body
Root chakra: Red

The angel meditation on the first day is with the angel of life, who gives us peace with the health of our body and also peace with what we do with our body. Our body is the physical vehicle for our soul and is designed to move—whether walking, working, creating, or participating in the numerous other actions we perform during our day. Our soul revels in our body because it moves.

The energy of the root chakra pertains to our get-up-and-go—our actions, enthusiasm for life, energy levels, and health and vitality, as well as our creative drive. Call on this angel at any time to purify, heal, and energise your body.

Why do we have a body?

Our body is a vehicle for our soul and the vehicle through which we express our soul's purpose. The Essenes believed we each have a purpose and a destiny to fulfil in our life. Our body is the instrument our soul inhabits so as to manifest our destiny.

If we did not have a physical body, nothing would actually happen. Our soul would still be floating above in the ethers, unable to ground its vision. We could have the most inspired dreams, but without our body, these dreams could not manifest. Our body is where the dreams of our soul and the love it wishes to express in the world are put into action. Our head, our heart, and our hands, are the three ways we give voice to our soul. A singer cannot sing, a mother cannot cook, and a builder cannot build without a body.

It is in our physical body that we get to experience life, and we are the envy of the angels because we live in physical form. The angels see the entire perspective of life from their vantage point—the present, past, and future. They see the whole world in the blink of an eye. We see life with human blinkers on; we find it hard to see the big picture and the journey of our soul.

We have even forgotten there is a master plan for our soul and that we chose our destiny before we were born. The angels know the master plan of our soul; they know our potential destiny. They know why we have chosen to incarnate into the body we have in this lifetime. The angels support us in the choices we make, the parents we choose, and the genetic heritage we are born into.

The Essenes emphasised the importance of healing and purification of the body, as they knew they were purifying the vehicle for the soul. They saw the body as an instrument of service. They wished to be of service to those around them, by teaching and healing. And they worked until very advanced ages with vigorous health. They believed they were here to make a positive difference for humanity, for those who lived in the same time frame as themselves and those who would live in the future. As their instruments of service, the bodies they inhabited were revered. They kept them as pure as possible with their angel meditations and purification practises.

The angels teach us to love and honour our body, as it is an expression of our soul. They teach us not to judge our body, as it is the perfect one for our soul in this lifetime. Life is a healing journey, as we all inherit genetic patterns that can manifest as health problems, either acute or chronic. Part of our own service is to heal these patterns of illness when they appear in our body. If we work to heal the patterns in our own body, we can clear them so they are less likely to manifest in future generations. The angel of life heals our body, and also the tendencies for illness we may have inherited from our ancestors, so we may create a more purified vehicle for our soul.

They described her as:

> The Angel of Life, she who gives strength and vigour to Man. For if the wax is not pure, how then can the candle give a steady flame? (*The Essene Gospel of Peace*)

The angel of life

The Essenes believed their brothers were the trees. Humanity is the pinnacle of evolution in the animal world, and trees are the pinnacles of evolution in the plant world. Trees stand as bastions to a time when we lived in harmony with the *being of the earth*. The trees are our brothers, and they are a living, breathing consciousness, acting as conduits for light and life force, channelling it deep within the earth herself.

> In the days of old, when the creation was young, the earth was filled with giant trees, whose branches soared above the clouds, and in them dwelled our ancient fathers, they who walked with the angels, and who lived by the holy law. In the shadow of their branches all men lived in peace. (*The Essene Gospel of Peace*)

Trees are a gift to the earth and to all of the creatures who live upon her surface. They are the lungs of the planet, and when they are in sufficient numbers, they will create balance in weather patterns. Trees stand as sentinels of time and bring about stability and harmony in the ecosystem. Tall trees form a canopy of protection for smaller trees and plants and are a haven for diverse creatures and insects.

The ancient trees have stood as witnesses to life on earth for generations; some may even have lived from the time of the Essenes. Trees have a singular relationship with time, as the years they have lived are encapsulated in their rings. Their rings tell us their age and how verdant those years were.

We can renew our relationship with time through trees. We can bring our thoughts, our feelings, and our bodies, together in one moment, instead of thinking about the future or the past as we so often do. The trunk of each tree is an anchor to the golden moment of now, the present moment, which is a place of peace. The more we can be in the present moment, the more peaceful we can feel. A practise we can cherish is to make the time to hug a tree. Be still and present with the tree, honouring it by wrapping our arms around it and breathing long and deeply as we lean against its trunk.

When we meet a tree in this way, we are gifted with a force of healing from the angel of life—who makes us strong as a tree, with roots anchoring us deep within the earth and a crown that reaches up to the sky. The angel of life gives us the abundant health we so desire. This is the angel who fills our body with health-giving life force and cleanses our body of impurities. We become strong and vital, healthy and whole:

> You will feel the power of the Angel of Life flow to your arms, and to your legs, and to all the parts of your body, as the sap flows in the tree in the spring, even as it runs out of the trunk. So will the Angel of Life flood your body with the power of the Mother Earth. (*The Essene Gospel of Peace*)

The earth is the supreme healer and we may receive her healing in a very simple way. All we need do is take off our shoes and walk barefoot on her surface. That is to walk on the grass, sand, or soil—not where the earth is covered with tarmac or concrete, or when our feet are in shoes, as these create barriers disconnect us from the earth.

Enlightened scientists have discovered that the earth resonates at a specific frequency of 7.83 Hz. This is known as the Schumann resonance, after the German scientist who discovered it. Science has also demonstrated that this is the natural frequency of the human body as well.

When we are barefoot on the earth, our body synchronously vibrates, like a tuning fork, at this same frequency of 7.83Hz. To harmonise in this way creates health and well-being and clears stress. If we are disconnected from the earth and this natural frequency, as we so often are in modern-day life, this leads to stress, illness, and chronic disease. To walk barefoot on the earth, for even half an hour a day, will attune us to the earth's natural, harmonic frequency, which manifests as reduced stress, greater relaxation, and improved health.

This is the science behind the teachings of many indigenous peoples and the Essenes. If we connect with nature and the earth, we will be more happy, healthy, and whole.

The angel of life brings healing, not only to ourselves but also to our ancestors. The angel of life knows our soul story. She knows who our ancestors were and where they lived on the earth. Each time we ask this angel for healing for ourselves, we also ask for healing for our ancestors. When we heal ourselves, we are healing those who have gone before.

> Those who have found peace with their body have built a sacred temple for the spirit. (*The Essene Gospel of Peace*)

Invite the angels of nature into your life

Angels are everywhere around us in nature. We breathe in the energy of angels on the air. We bathe in the energy of angels as we swim. We bask in the energy of the angels as we walk in the sun. The Essenes believed the elements that make up our world are angels—the sun, the air, and the water are angels. We are surrounded, in each moment, by the energy and the consciousness of angels.

The angels are not removed from our lives, existing somewhere detached from our reality in higher realms. Every day we are living in the realm of the angels. They are an intrinsic part of nature, and we are infused with their energy with each breath we take. The Essenes believed there were three angels of nature who were especially significant for our personal healing. These were the angel of air, the angel of water, and the angel of the sun, all of which are angels of the Mother Earth. These are the three angels invoked by the Essenes to cleanse and purify their bodies.

The wind and the breeze is the angel of air. This is the same element we breathe in and that gives us life. The angel of air is a gift from the Mother Earth:

Then shall you breathe long and deeply, that the
Angel of Air may be brought within you. (*The
Essene Gospel of Peace*)

We can receive the healing of the angel of air by asking this
angel to flow into our body with our breath—healing our body
and refreshing our blood, clearing stagnant thoughts and stale
energy. We can open our windows and ask the angel of air to
come into our home and to cleanse and refresh our living space.
This angel brings healing to our outer space, our home, and our
inner space, our body.

The angel of water is in the rain, the rivers, and the oceans.
The Essenes would bathe in the rivers to cleanse their bodies. Or
when they lived in their temples in the mountains, they would
bathe in ritual baths. This practise of water purification with the
angels was one reason they lived to such extraordinary ages.

We can bathe in the ocean ourselves or in a safe place in a
river, as here we are in touch with the angels of nature. We can
even have a new intention when we bathe or shower at home,
imagining the angel of water cleansing and purifying our body.

We can drink water infused with the angels by blessing the
water before we drink it, inviting the angel of water to infuse
every drop with its healing energy and love. We will then imbibe
consciousness-rich water and life force into every cell of our body.
The angels simply wait to be asked, and in faith, we only have
to ask once.

The third angel of nature is the angel of the sun. The sun
is the giver of life. And yet, we have become afraid of the sun,
hiding behind dark glasses and smearing lotions on our skin.
There would be no life on this planet without the light and
warmth of the sun.

The angel of the sun can heal and purify our body, cleansing
it with a spiritual fire. Ask the angel of the sun to flow into your
body and warm it with its rays. The angel of the sun is always

present, even when the sun is behind the clouds, we can still receive the healing of the angel of the sun.

These are the three angels of the Mother Earth, who give healing to our body.

> When he who suffers with pains and grievous plague asks for your help … tell him to invoke the Angel of the Sun, the Angel of Water, and the Angel of Air, that they may enter his body. (The Essene *Gospel of Peace*)

Honour our body with our food, and we honour the earth

Incredibly the Essenes lived up to 140 years old, whilst living vibrantly and purposefully and being of service to others. They invoked the angels into everything they did—into their healing, their meditations, their work, and their daily lives. They lived close to nature, and their lives were a sacrament to the angels. They lived in joy because they knew and respected the invisible world of the angels. To the Essenes, to live consciously with the angels was to live a life of fulfilment and happiness.

The Essenes lived to great ages because they ate fresh, living food, full of life force. They ate a raw diet of sprouted grains and fruit in summer and dried fruit and nuts and some milk from their sheep in winter. To the Essenes, everything they ate was a gift from the Mother Earth.

The food of the Essenes not only contained minerals, vitamins, and other nutrients; it also contained the key ingredient of life force. Their food was tended and nurtured by the angels as it grew and was infused with the healing energies of the angels of the sun, water, air, and earth.

Our food may look bright and colourful, but the invisible

ingredient of life force is often absent. If food has been stored, frozen, chilled, or dried, the food is no longer living food, as it is devoid of life force. The food we buy on the supermarket shelves would be considered nearly dead by the Essenes, and according to the Essenes, dead food created ill health and disease. In our modern society, we have become used to having diverse fruits and vegetables available for most of the year. Our food is often stored for long periods of time in packets or tins and even frozen.

The Essenes lived to such extraordinary ages because their food was abundant with life force and the healing energy of the angels. They ate fresh food according to each season and always harvested the food just prior to each meal. They stored their excess food for winter by drying it with the angels in the sun. We can ask the angels to infuse our food with their hidden and sacred ingredient, as this is the magical force that will infuse our body with its healing powers as we eat.

The Essenes grew their food in cocreative partnership with the angels. The soil was infused with the warmth of the angel of the sun. The moisture in the soil was alive with the energy of the angel of water. The angel of air kept the soil friable, allowing the soil and the roots of the plants to breathe. These three angels all play in the soil, which is the realm of the angel of earth. This is the angel who tends the soil, the womb of our Mother Earth, as she gives life and food to those who live on her surface.

We can imagine ourselves standing upon the earth, like a tree, with our roots deep within the soil, sustained by all the angels of the Mother Earth. We can envision free-flowing life force coursing through our body, like the sap does through a tree, bringing health and healing to every cell in our body.

Conscious Gardening

> Celebrate a daily feast of the gifts of the Angel of
> the Earth.
>
> —*The Essene Gospel of Peace.*

The Essenes were conscious gardeners. They ate food imbued with the energies of the earth and her angels. This, combined with their purification practises, made them an extraordinary people. They were healthy and productive in their work until a very advanced age.

It is possible for us to learn from the Essenes and the angels and bring some of their teachings into our own lives. If we are fortunate enough to own a garden, we can see it with new eyes and with new possibilities of cocreative gardening with the angels.

This is a complete paradigm shift from the gardening and farming with man-made chemicals that is so commonplace in our modern world. The gardening of the Essenes was designed to create life and health. We have digressed from this so far as to create food that is toxic and infiltrated with chemicals.

Even if we cannot directly affect the modern world of agriculture, we are empowered to make a difference to the food we can grow ourselves. We can garden more consciously by asking for the assistance of the angels of nature. We can invite in the angel of the sun, the angel of water, the angel of air, and the angel of earth, whether we are weeding and digging the soil, sowing the seeds, or harvesting our produce. The Essenes created a garden in a desert because they gardened with the angels.

If we do not have our own garden, maybe we can sow some herbs or lettuce in pots, so we may then have some consciously grown, life force-infused food to eat. The angels are still present, even in the cities, and if you ask, they will come close as you prepare the soil, sow the seeds and tend the plants as they grow. The angels ask us to pick the food with love, as it is the small things that matter most, and this love will go into the food we then eat.

The Essenes were essentially raw food fruitarians. They taught that, to eat a raw, plant-based diet was nature's healing gift to our body. They ate kindly, as they believed this was in alignment with the One Law by which they lived. To eating anything that had been killed was considered out of alignment with the One Law of Nature. They ate food in season, as this is what nature intended, and any excess fruit was dried in the sun and stored for winter.

We learn from the Essenes to honour our food. And we learn from them to eat with love and gratitude, however simple the meal may be. They invoked the angel of water and the angel of air as they ate. They ate in silence, chewing every mouthful with care. If we can honour our food by giving it our full attention, then we are honouring the earth and all of her angels.

We have become quite removed from the Essene way of living and eating consciously. To begin to honour our food, we can begin by turning off our phones and screens while we eat and giving our food our full attention. We can create a quiet space, where we can be present with our food—a simple, sacred space for our mealtimes.

We can give thanks to the angels and the Mother Earth for their abundance Even if our food has not been prepared by ourselves and was grown with no awareness of the angels, we may still give thanks, silently and inwardly, as the angels hear our thoughts. Gratitude is a transformative feeling. To be grateful for the small pleasures in life is a quality of the angels, and gratitude creates joy.

If we can create a space to grow some of our own food, we can reconnect with the cycles of nature—the rhythm of the year and the seasons. The angels have different roles during the varying seasons of the year. In the winter, they work deep in the earth, healing and renewing her core. During spring and summer, their energies ascend, bringing vigour and lushness to the new year's food.

Healing

> When the Mother Earth's angels enter into your body ... then shall all uncleanness depart in haste, and your blood shall become as pure as our Mother Earth's blood ... Your breath as pure as the breath of fragrant flowers, your flesh as pure as the flesh of fruits ripening upon the leaves of trees, the light of your eye as clear and bright as the brightness of the sun shining upon the blue sky.
>
> —*The Essene Gospel of Peace*

The Essenes were known as gifted healers. They healed with the angels and prescribed herbs, fasting, and prayer. When someone came to them who was sick, they recommended a seven-day fast. They taught the sick person how to invoke the angels of the sun, water, and air for their healing. After seven days of being with the angels, the person was completely transformed and healed, often in miraculous ways.

Once the person was healed, they made certain recommendations to maintain his or her newfound health. Only eat two or three types of food at one meal and always stop eating before feeling full. They taught the person how to make their Essene bread—how to sprout the wheat, which was moistened with water, in a small container in the sun and then to invoke the angel of the sun, the angel of water, and the angel of air, who would bring their energy to the sprouting and growth of the seed. Once the seed had germinated, it was crushed and moulded into wafers, and these were also dried in the sun with the angels. This was living, "angel-infused" food and a staple of the Essene diet.

We can be inspired by the angel of life to give life and health to our body. We can do so with the food we eat, the water we drink, and the air we breathe; our body is made out of what we take into our body. The gift of peace with our body is the first of the gifts of the angels. This peace may be the most tangible, as our body, when ill, can be in pain or distress. Our body is our gift of life from the angels and especially from the angel of life. We can call on this angel to bring peace and healing to our body—the first of the peace that is sevenfold.

> Long ago, before the great flood, the great ones walked the earth. The giant trees, even those which now are no more than legend, were their home and their kingdom. They lived many scores of generations, for they ate from the table of the Mother Earth and slept in the arms of the Divine. They knew no disease, old age or death.
>
> —*The Essene Gospel of Peace*

Angel of Power

Chapter 5

Day Two, Monday
Angel of Power

Angel invocation

> "I ask the Angel of Peace to always be with me,
> and I ask the Angel of Power to help me feel more
> peaceful in my thoughts."
> —*The Essene Gospel of Peace*

The gift of the angel of power: Peace with our mind
Sacral Chakra: Orange

The angel on the second day is the angel of power. This
angel guides us to feel more peaceful with our thoughts and our
feelings.

A whole world goes on inside us, which no one else sees
or hears, as our thoughts are silent. Those who know us well
may be aware when we are caught up in our inner world by our
facial expressions or moods, however we try to hide them. We
cannot hide our thoughts, and the angels know this. Even though
our thoughts are invisible, they create an energy that is felt by
everyone. As the ancient Essenes believed, "No man is an island."
Every one of our thoughts affects everyone around us.

We have conscious thoughts, those we are aware of. And we
also have unconscious thoughts. These are the thoughts that lurk
in the shadows, which have lingered from our past. We think that,
because we are not consciously thinking of past events anymore,

they have passed and we have moved on, but the memories are stored in the deeper recesses of our subconscious mind.

We also inherit thought patterns from our parents and ancestors. These thought patterns are often very familiar to us, and we think they are our own. But they have travelled down through the DNA of our ancestors for many generations. Without knowing it, we repeat the patterns of our ancestors. We respond and react to situations in often very similar ways our forebears did.

We learn as children how to behave and how to hone our mental and emotional responses from our parents or those who have raised us. We may be taught consciously, but we also learn via unconscious observation, almost by osmosis, the emotional and mental habits of our parents. Our parents or guardians can only teach us the emotional skills they have inherited or learned from their own parents. The cycle of unconscious patterns, both negative and positive, will continue from one generation to the next, unless we wake up to the possibility that we can change and heal.

Both our conscious and subconscious memories and our patterns of behaviour may need healing. This is where we can ask for assistance from the angels, and especially the angel of power.

Call on this angel to feel more peaceful in your inner world. The angel of power lovingly helps us to heal any thoughts or feelings that are troubling us, so we may let go of any outdated thoughts from the past. We are now in a time where we may move on and embrace a new beginning for ourselves, with a clear head and a strong heart.

On the second day, the angels purify our sacral chakra. When cleansed and purified, the sacral chakra is the place of our highest spiritual achievement and our ultimate creativity. The job in hand is to cleanse our sacral chakra of our negative thoughts and feelings. This cleansing process is the foundation of our spiritual growth.

The sacral chakra contains the heights of our potential and

the depths of our inner world. It is here where we store all the negative thoughts and experiences from our past that are in need of healing. The angels are here to support us in what may seem a huge task, to heal and cleanse the deeper recesses of our soul. With the love of the angels, we can heal, without judgement or fear, any thoughts and experiences from anytime in our past. This is the beginning of inner peace.

Our thoughts are like air

Our thoughts are like air. They are invisible and without boundaries. But unknown to us, our thoughts also have an invisible impact. We think our thoughts are contained within our minds but this is not so. Our thoughts, as soon as we think them, fly free from our body. To the ancient Essenes, our thoughts travelled on the wind and infused the air that we breathe.

When we think a thought, it flies free on the wind, moving quickly around the planet. Negative thoughts are deafening energetically and can reap huge destruction. They can create gentle breezes, strong winds, and even damaging storms. We think that because our thoughts are contained within our mind that no one hears them.

But each one of our thoughts creates an energy, and even if a thought is not spoken as words, there is still a huge energy behind it. Just because we do not feel the storm created by a negative thought or the fragrant breeze created by a positive thought does not mean it is not happening. Our "silent" thoughts are heard loudly and clearly in the invisible realm of the angels.

In daily life, we may sense the energy of thoughts as an atmosphere. We may have had an experience of walking into a room and having a feeling such as, *This feels nice; it's warm and cosy*, even with no one else there. Or conversely, the thought could have been, *It feels really unpleasant in here*, and you feel you do not want to stay. What we have felt is the energy of past thoughts, as thoughts do not disappear; they linger in the atmosphere, creating a tangible atmosphere and energy.

The salutary lesson is that the energy of thoughts remains in the place in which they were thought, to be met again later by those visiting that place. We do not realise this, but it's true. Happy, kind people thinking happy, kind thoughts create a warm and relaxed atmosphere—somewhere we want to stay. Those who argue and who think aggressive, unhappy thoughts create an inhospitable and unfriendly atmosphere. They create places where we obviously do not want to stay. Even though the negative thoughts may have ceased quite some time before, the energy is still tangible in the air.

The angels encourage us to wake up to the power of our thoughts. As soon as we have thought a thought, it flies free from the confines of our mind, never to return.

The Essenes believed our thoughts create *beings*—in other words, an "energy." They wished to create positive and lightful beings, so they invoked the angels into every one of their thoughts. Hence not only the thought but also the energy of the thought was beautiful. This positive energy will then travel around the planet, felt as harmonious and loving energy by all beings:

> For we do not think of the angel of air when we breathe, for we breathe without thought, as the sons of darkness live their lives without thought.
> (*The Essene Gospel of Peace*)

The air we breathe

The first thing we do when we are born is start to breathe. The breath is life, and we only live because we breathe. We can live without water for up to a few days and may survive for longer without food, maybe for several days, but we can only live for a few minutes without air. Every creature—whether human, animal, bird, fish, or plant—that lives on the earth breathes the same air. We share the air that gives us life. It circulates and recirculates, through countless living creatures, the trees, and even the plankton in the oceans.

There is only one element of air, and it has no boundaries. It is not like the element of earth, with all of its rocks and stones and grains of sand, all with their solid boundaries. Nor is it like the water in the creeks, rivers, and oceans, all of which flow contained within the natural depressions on the Earth. Air is completely free to flow wherever it wishes. There is only one body of air that touches and interconnects every living thing.

The ancient Essenes revered the element of air above all of the other elements of nature. They believed the element of air extended beyond the atmosphere of the earth. Even though, high up, it is not air we can breathe, they believed it connected us with untold planets and stars. The element of air connects us with the visible and also the invisible. There is a mysterious quality to the air we breathe. As it connects us with all of the beings in all of the different realms of creation, the breath connects us with the angels.

To the Essenes the breath was the most sacred of the elements. It was often known as the Holy Breath or even the Holy Spirit. The breath was considered to be a mystery, as there is an unseen, spiritual quality to the breath.

In the Essene language of Aramaic, the word for the breath and the Holy Spirit is one and the same—*Ruha*. The Ruha is the mysterious go-between, or connection between ourselves and the Divine. Our breath and our spirit are one. To breathe is to connect with our own inner spirit, or the Holy Spirit as it was known by the Essenes—which is everywhere around us and also within us. This is our connection to the Divine. This is the spiritual nature of the breath, of the element of air, which was so revered by the Essenes. The breath is the omnipresent spirit, being breathed, and giving life to all living beings.

The air we breathe is a mystery of the Divine. The air is invisible, and yet we feel its touch upon our face. We see the leaves bend in the breeze, but we do not see the hand that moves them. We hear the sound of the wind in the trees, but the wind itself is soundless unless it touches something. This is the mystery of the air and the breath. Its effects are seen and heard, yet of itself, it is unseen and unheard. The wind and the air are our tangible, and intangible, connection with the ethereal world, the world of spirit.

If we can open ourselves to perceive from a more sensitive place, the mystery of air may reveal itself. When it does, we can see that the air is filled with sacred letters. These letters eddy and flow in the wind as spiritual entities, each letter made of light and having a specific form. As they fly on the wind, these letters of light embody the pattern and order of creation. They are the language of light of the Divine, which we are able to see once our perception is opened to the realm of the angels and the mysteries of life. The angel of air is the doorway to the inner mystery, connecting us with our soul and our true divine nature. With the angel of air, we can feel the breath of our spirit as it flows in and out of our body.

In the words of the Essenes:

> In the moment between the breathing in and the breathing out are hidden all of the mysteries. (*The Essene Gospel of Peace*)

The Essenes understood the mystery of the breath and taught that the breath is our key to peace. We can ask the angel of air to help us be more mindful and conscious of our breathing, as this will lead to the inner peace everyone craves. We take our breath and our breathing for granted, but if we can be more conscious of our breath, as it flows in and out of our body, we will begin to feel more peaceful.

We breathe in our body, and it is only our body that lives fully in the present moment, as often, our thoughts project into the future or dwell on the past. If our thoughts are focussed on the past or the future, we are not fully present in our body.

As our body is an anchor to the present, to the eternal moment of *now*, if we can be more conscious of our breathing, we can be more fully present in our body. We can let go of thinking about the past or the future, and we can begin to feel more peaceful. To breathe peacefully is to breathe deep into the belly, relaxing the diaphragm and organs. The belly is the place of the sacral energy centre, the focus of this angel meditation with the angel of power.

To purify our sacral chakra is the foundation of our spiritual growth; it is a necessary part of our spiritual process. The angel of power purifies our sacral chakra of our negative thoughts and feelings, so that we may manifest our spiritual creativity and inspiration from our soul. To manifest the potential we have as we purify this chakra is the pinnacle of our spiritual achievement.

One with the earth

The earth is a living being. She is sentient and conscious, and as such, she has a planetary mind and also a planetary feeling body. She knows where each one of us is on the planet at any one moment in time.

We are intimately connected and completely interdependent with the earth. We are not separate. The ego of humanity has led us to believe that we can take from the earth whatever we wish, and it will not affect her. We have believed, and many still do, that we can pollute the earth with no ill effect. This has happened because we have thought we are separate. This is the mistaken belief of a distorted human ego.

We are one with the earth, and this is not purely on a material level. We are one with the earth because what we think and what we feel also affects the earth.

We each have our own individual mind, and the earth has her own mind, the planetary mind. We each have our own individual feelings, and the earth has her own feelings, her emotional body. We each have our own individual physical body, and the earth has her own body—this beautiful blue, green planet upon which we live.

What each one of us thinks affects every other person on the planet. These thoughts also affect the earth herself, as the collective mind of humanity and the mind of the earth are one mind. We are not separate.

What each one of us feels affects every other person upon the planet. These feelings also affect the being of the earth, as she feels what we feel too. The earth is sensitive to what we feel, both as individuals and as a collective of humanity.

The angels ask us to be more conscious of what we think, as it affects all of those around us and also the earth herself. If we can awaken to this awareness, it can be something quite beautiful, which we have been unaware of for so long. We can begin to live our lives more consciously aware of the earth and honour her as a sentient being too.

Weather makers

> But mankind does not see the carnage, nor does he hear the piteous cries of his victims, for he is blind to the world of spirit.
>
> —*The Essene Gospel of Peace*

The unseen realms feel the impact of our thoughts. Just because we cannot see the invisible world does not mean that it is unaffected. Once we have thought a thought, it can never be destroyed. This is the power of our thoughts and why we invoke the angel of power for guidance with our thoughts.

Once we think a thought, it flies free to affect all living beings, wherever they live on the planet. Our thoughts also affect the weather; unbeknown to us, we are weather makers. The Essenes believed our thoughts affect the element of air, and the collective thoughts of humanity amass together to influence the winds and the breeze. Soft and gentle thoughts will create soft and gentle breezes, but powerfully negative thoughts can amass together to create a wind so strong as to be a storm.

The collective thoughts of humanity impact the planetary mind of the earth, and she attempts to rebalance the equilibrium of her body, our home, through the weather. Extreme winds and storms are an expression of imbalances within the collective human psyche, which negatively impact upon the living earth, Gaia.

The earth feels what we feel, and where the earth particularly resonates with our emotions is in the element of water. Where the element of air resonates with our thoughts, the element of water resonates with our feelings. All of the water upon the planet acts like a tuning fork, resonating with the collective emotions of humanity. Soft and gentle feelings will create soft and gentle rains. The tumultuous collective emotions of humanity fall as the torrents of lashing rain in their attempt to cleanse the earth. Our emotional body and the earth's emotional body is one body. We cry our own tears to heal our emotions, and the earth cries her tears too.

We are weather makers; we have the power to shape our world. With the love and guidance of the angels, we can begin to take responsibility for our thoughts and our feelings.

Time for change

To take responsibility for our thoughts is to become peacemakers, and this is the first step towards creating peace on the planet. Peace begins with each one of us as individuals, as peace begins within.

It can appear challenging because our thoughts can seem so strong. Strong thoughts can create equally strong feelings, which may feel as though we are riding huge waves on a stormy ocean. When we feel a maelstrom of thoughts and emotions, it can be all encompassing and completely consuming.

But there is a window of opportunity when the light goes on and we can think to ourselves, *I am thinking the same old negative thoughts. I am doing this again.* We can become aware of a familiar repetitive pattern. Change begins with self-realisation—with *I am thinking this again.* And then we may ask ourselves the question, *How may I change this?* The answer is that the change we wish to have is possible if we invite the angels into our lives.

The angels are waiting to help us. They do not expect us to do this alone. Living more consciously is as simple and beautiful as inviting the angels into our life. They wait in the wings as wise, compassionate observers, knowing the moment will come when we will invite in their presence.

We are the ultimate creative beings, and our collective soul destiny is to create a paradise on earth, as cocreators with the angels. Each individual human light will one day turn on, and our soul destiny, individually and collectively, is to create a paradise on earth. We have journeyed through a long and dark time, incarnating numerous times in many places upon this planet and others—often experiencing challenging soul experiences, all of which are designed for our greater soul growth.

Now is a time for change, as we are travelling back towards the light. The light the earth is travelling towards is that of the galactic sun. This differs from the sun we see in the sky. This is the sun that sits at the centre of our galaxy. The galactic sun has been revered by the ancients since time immemorial. It is a spiritual source of light for our planet and also a source of love. The journey we have been on, as a collective, has been one of a loss of love. We are now entering a new phase, a new beginning for love, for ourselves, for each other, and for the planet. This is why the angels are more present at this time, as we are turning the corner to begin to love ourselves again.

Angel of power

> There is no greater power in heaven and earth
> than the thoughts of humanity.
> —*The Essene Gospel of Peace*

We invoke the angel of power to gift us with peace with our thoughts. We do not realise how powerful we are. We have forgotten how to take responsibility for our thoughts. We think that, as long as we do not say what we think or act on what we think, then it is acceptable. But our thoughts are powerful, and the effects know no boundaries, as they are carried on the wind.

In the Essene tradition, the initiate had to study for seven years before he or she was given the knowledge of the angels. This was because the Essenes understood the strength of the power of our thoughts. They believed that the initiate had to complete certain levels of self-mastery before being given the secrets of the angels.

We are supremely powerful beings, and to quote the words of Marianne Williamson, as spoken by Nelson Mandela, "Our deepest fear is not that we are inadequate. Our deepest fear is that we are powerful beyond measure. It is our light, not our darkness that most frightens us."

The angel of power encourages us to be wise and kind in our thoughts. It is the power of our thoughts that creates our feelings and also our actions. We can invoke the angel of power into everything we do, both big and small—even how we turn a door handle or how we smile at someone we hardly know.

To invoke this angel into all our thoughts is to infuse every little action we do with the love of the Divine. We become an instrument of divine love. Life may seem mundane at times, but it can be transformed if we put our love into the little things. Magic happens if we focus on the details, and even everyday tasks become joyful.

Angel of wisdom

> For with your thoughts guided by holy Wisdom,
> humanity builds a bridge of light to reach God.
> —*The Essene Gospel of Peace*

Power and love are the two sides of the same coin. They are inextricably linked. In the Essene teachings, they are the two wings of a bird. One wing is power, and the other wing is love. The analogy is that we are each a bird. We have wings, but we have yet to learn to fly. The angel of wisdom is the one that teaches us to learn to fly. If we are wise with our power and compassionate in our love, then we can unfurl our wings and fly to spiritual heights.

This is a gift of the angel of wisdom, who helps us go beyond ordinary thinking. Our truly spiritual thoughts come not from our own mind but are divinely inspired. They come from a deeper and more spiritual source within us.

As we feel more peaceful in our thoughts, we create a space inside us where something else can come through—something of a higher vibration, which is of the essence of love. This is the wisdom of the Divine. To be in touch with this divine wisdom is when we create beautiful beings with our thoughts. This is when we connect with our spiritual source of creativity and when the energy that flows from within the confines of our mind is felt as the touch of grace from above.

This flow of spiritual thought is experienced as thought "without thinking." When we can let go of the "monkey mind," our overbusy minds, we can connect with a different kind of thought. This is peaceful thought. It is divinely inspired thought, and it happens in the quiet times.

Practise the angel meditation every day. Ask the angel of wisdom to create peace in your thinking, and this angel will open the door to divine inspiration. It feels like effortless thought, connecting with a source of wisdom beyond knowing. The thoughts flow with complete integrity. There is a sense of deep peace and happiness, of being in tune with something greater— divine flow, divine wisdom.

This is a gift of our true inheritance and a gift from the angels. It's our gift to unwrap as we wake up and take responsibility for ourselves and our thoughts. Don't expect to get it right all of the time, as we are all on our human journey, with all of our frailties and vulnerabilities. We are relearning something we knew a very long time ago. We have forgotten about our angel friends and how they may help us. We believed we were separate from our unseen friends. Now, as our soul memory returns, it is time to remember:

> The longer you walk with the angels and keep their Law, the stronger your thoughts become in sacred Wisdom. (*The Essene Gospel of Peace*)

Freeing ourselves

Peace on the second day pertains to the sacral chakra, our ultimate creative energy centre. We have such potential as human beings, but we have work to do. We need to spring-clean the

45

cupboards of our unconscious mind. This is especially pertinent when it comes to the sacral energy centre, as here we operate mostly unconsciously. The sacral centre is the realm of the subconscious and unconscious mind.

It takes practise to create peace with our thinking, as our thoughts are so powerful and are even addictive. We often find ourselves in repetitive negative patterns of thought because they come from that unconscious place within us.

We consider ourselves to be independent, free-thinking individuals. But in reality, we are not. We are bound by our conditioned patterns, which come from different streams; our ancestral genetic lineage, which we inherit from our parents; our karmic conditioned patterns, from our soul lineage; and our connection with the collective unconscious of humanity.

The angels are here to heal the bonds that keep us tied to these patterns, which are like chains around our mind. Even though these chains are invisible they are immensely strong. This is why we ask the angel of power to help us, not only with our conscious thoughts but also with the thoughts we are not conscious of. Our unconscious thoughts and attitudes are the ones that drive us, as they are the compost out of which our conscious thoughts grow. It is our unconscious thoughts and attitudes that can keep us in a self-limiting reality. The angel of power is the angel who "breaks the bonds of death," so we may release ourselves from the chains which imprison us in our self-limiting beliefs. The angel of power is the one who will set us free.

To be really free is a process of personal healing and transformation. If we consider the number of people behind us in our ancestral lineage, it doubles every generation. If we go back just ten generations it is over one thousand people, 99 per cent of whom we have never known. We might be lucky and have photographs that extend back four generations, or we may have names on a family tree that extend back a little further. But most of our ancestors who we inherit our DNA from are strangers to us. We do not even know their names.

It's important to realise that our DNA doesn't just give us the colour of our eyes and hair or the health of our body. It also gives to us our attitudes and the way we think. People who are natives of various countries can have distinctly differing attitudes and ways of thinking. We may say someone is very British or French or Peruvian. This is not only perpetuated by the language, the culture, and upbringing; it is also imprinted upon the DNA that each person inherits.

Attitudes can be formative at a national level, and at a more personal level, attitudes can be unique within individual family groups. These are the inherited attitudes that have been in our respective genetic lineages for generations. We all have layers of conditioned thoughts and attitudes, with their sources being familial and national, the various substrata within our societies, and also the collective unconscious of humanity.

Our attitudes shape our thinking. Our attitudes lie deep within us and are the bedrock from which our conscious thoughts spring. As well as inheriting mental attitudes from our ancestors, our formative childhood years are pivotal in how we form our attitudes and thought processes, and these will influence us throughout our life.

Our thought patterns are also seeded in our experiences while we are growing in our mother's womb. We can feel the thoughts and the feelings of our mother, and as thoughts and feelings create biological chemicals, these flow into our developing body-mind system as an unborn child—laying the foundations for the learned responses of our thoughts and feelings during our life. We are highly influenced by our subconscious and unconscious conditioning. It is as though we have been programmed, and we do not realise it.

Every cell in our body has memory, and every cell in our body has intelligence. Modern-day holistic health talks about the body-mind system. The body and the mind are not separate; they are one functioning unit. Every event that happens to us during our lifetime is encoded within our cellular memory—from present experiences, to as far back as our childhood and in utero experience. Our experiences in past lives are also encoded within our aura, chakras, and the cells of our body as energetic memories. Who we are and what we experience in our life is the consequence of everything that has gone before. This is called our karma.

We are the envy of the angels because we live in a physical body. The body we live in and the family we are born into is all a chosen soul experience. It is part of our karmic destiny. On a soul level, we chose our parents before we were conceived. And if we believe that, then it follows that we also chose our DNA. Whatever our chosen soul experience is, we always have an experience through which we can learn and to grow. We can think of ourselves as compost. If we look after the compost and water it with the angel of water and keep it warm with the angel of the sun, we can grow into a beautiful flowering plant.

The angels know why we have chosen our particular family to be born into. They know it is a chosen soul experience, with all of its gifts and challenges. The angels are here to help us manifest our greatest potential, whatever situation we find ourselves in.

With the love of the angels, we can step forward and say yes to change. Even though we may not know the big picture of our karmic journey, we can ask the angel of power to release us from the chains that hold us back. The bonds have served their purpose, and it is now time to let them go, with gratitude and with love.

At times, we are troubled by thinking negatively. As we begin to be more conscious of ourselves, we can become more aware of the patterns of our thinking. There will be moments when we will catch ourselves in a negative mindset. These can be repetitive thoughts, which can trap us into a negative vortex. With the love of the angels, we can lovingly let go of any negative thoughts from any time—even the conditioned, unconscious thoughts we didn't even know existed. All thoughts are only energy, and we can let go of anything with the love of the angels.

We can also invite the angels into our home or workplace, as negative thoughts can gather in the atmosphere of where we live or work. We can cleanse the energy of any space by simply opening the windows and inviting in the angel of air. This angel will bring fresh new energy into your environment—at the same time whisking away any negative thoughts, which can be seen as negative energies floating in the atmosphere.

The angel of air is profoundly cleansing and is intimately connected with the angel of wisdom. The angel of wisdom, whose natural home is upon the element of air, guides our thoughts. Both of these angels bring healing to all people and to the Mother Earth herself, so that she may be cleansed of the negative thought patterns of humanity that have accumulated in her atmosphere.

One drop in the ocean

Our unconscious mind is not only contained within ourselves, but also extends to include every other human being upon the planet. This is known as the collective unconscious of humanity. It is an unconscious, global mind, with each one of us as a neuron in its structure. We are all equally affected by this collective mind. We think we operate as individuals, as separate units, but we do not, as we are all intricately connected via this collective unconscious mind.

The collective unconscious is often thought of as an ocean. We, as human beings, are comprised of 70 per cent water, and as we are mainly water, we are profoundly affected by the effects of the collective. We can imagine each one of us as being a drop of water in an ocean of collective consciousness. And as the water flows, all of the individual drops of water flow in the same direction as the current. We are all part of this human, global mind, and we are all affected by this global mind because we are each one drop in its collective ocean. We contribute to it with our own thoughts, and we are affected by it as a consequence of the thoughts of others.

In one way this phenomenon has been a prison, which we have been unaware of. In another, it is our path to freedom because it is through the collective that we can particularly connect with the angels. As we invite the angels into our lives, we begin to lives our life more consciously.

Imagine each drop of water waking up and becoming more conscious of its thoughts and feelings. As one drop in the ocean of the collective, we can each make a difference, because we are all connected to every other drop in the ocean. As we begin to think more peaceful thoughts, this same peace radiates out to affect all the other drops, so that they too may begin to feel more peaceful. This is an expression of the power of the individual.

We are so much more powerful than we believe or even understand at this point in time. We are taking baby steps towards a new beginning, which is new dawn for humanity and the earth, one of living with more conscious self-awareness, of remembering that we are all connected through the collective unconscious. It's a time where we may begin to reclaim our true spiritual power and live as conscious cocreators with the angels. We are brilliant, creative beings, and the angels know this is our potential.

We can call on the angel of wisdom to support us with our thinking, and remind us to love ourselves as we are, because we are perfect as we are. We chose our ancestral lineage and our patterns of thinking as a soul lesson for this incarnation. We can say to ourselves these words: "I love myself as I am, and there is nothing I need to change."

The ultimate wisdom is to love ourselves as we are and to let go of judging ourselves. We are the envy of the angels because we experience life in physical form, and they do not judge us.

We need to remember to laugh at ourselves—to not take life so seriously but to bring humour into our lives. The angels live on the vibration of joy, and with joy comes compassion.

We may fail to "get it right" all of the time, as that is part of the human journey. The angels encourage us to enjoy our newfound mindfulness, be light, and enjoy each moment. They encourage us to know that we are making a difference simply because we are coming from the highest intention, and we have begun our awakening journey with the angels.

> When the power of thought is guided by Sacred Wisdom, then the thoughts of the Son of Man lead him to build a paradise on Earth.
>
> —*The Essene Gospel of Peace*

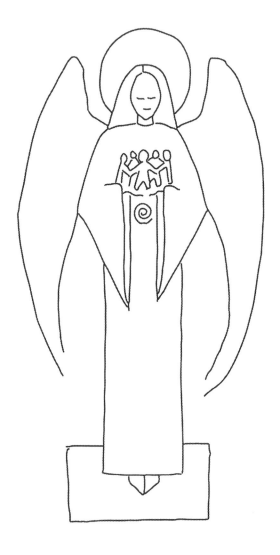

Angel of love

Chapter 6

Day Three, Tuesday
Angel of Love

Angel invocation

> I ask the Angel of Peace to always be with me,
> and I ask the Angel of Love to bring peace and
> harmony to my family.
>
> —*The Essene Gospel of Peace*

The gift of the angel of love: Peace with our family
Solar plexus chakra: Yellow

The angel on the third day is the angel of love, whose gift to
us is peace with our feelings. The Essenes taught about love. The
purpose of their life with the angels was to live a life of love. Love
was the essence of their teaching. They had many great teachers
who left their community and taught about love. They even
travelled the world to teach about love. The love of the Essenes
was an all-encompassing love, the love of the Mother Earth and
her creatures and plants and the love of each other and their fellow
man. Their love was a divinely inspired love.

The angel of love heals our feelings. The Essenes would
invoke the angel of love to fill their hearts with love for their
family and to heal any discord that might arise. They believed
this angel was the most important, as the angel of love heals the
suffering in peoples' lives. They believed many people suffer and

that suffering is part of the human experience. We suffer because we do not feel loved, or we do not believe we are worthy of love.

The angel of love brings a deep healing to anything that is "unlove." Unlove is the opposite of love. It is a lack or an absence of love, in either the giving or the receiving of love. In its extreme, unlove is hate or anger, but it is any experience of not feeling loved by another or of not feeling loved by ourselves.

The angel of love brings the much-needed gift of love for ourselves and our family. It heals all family discord, whether trivial or major and spreads love as a balm to sooth our emotions. It is a love of unconditional acceptance for ourselves and for others.

We feel gentler and more loving as we invoke the Angel of Love. We learn to respond instead of reacting, finding a new and peaceful way to relate. We feel we deserve to both give and receive love. Our relationships flourish. We feel whole and complete as we heal all that is unlove inside us. The child we once were feels loved and secure, as our inner child is always within us. So much of our need for love is the cry of our inner child for love.

Love is gentle and also strong. With the angel of love, we feel we are loved and secure, both loving and lovable. We can learn to love and accept ourselves as we are, to know there is nothing we need to change, as we are already perfect as we are.

★★★

> Without love, a Man's heart is parched and cracked as the bottom of a dry well, and his words are empty as a hollow gourd. But loving words are as a honeycomb, sweet to the soul.
> —*The Essene Gospel of Peace*

Love is the essence of life, the weft and warp of creation. Love came before everything that was ever created. With the angels, we will journey back to love, as the angel of love will heal everything within us that is unlove.

The Essenes believed water is a gift of love from the angels. The angel of water and the angel of love are a pair of angels who work together, as all of the water on the planet is an expression of the angel of love. We are conceived and we grow in the warm waters of our mother's womb. As it is a place inherently full of love, the water we grow in is love. We are born from an ocean of love.

As watery beings, we are able to feel emotions as they resonate around us. Our experience of love or unlove began in the womb, as we felt our mother's emotions as our emotions; whatever she felt we felt. If our mother felt love, we felt love. If our mother felt sad, then we felt sad. Our mother, the earth, feels what we feel too. We are intrinsically one with both of our mothers—the mother we grew in and our mother the earth.

Our feelings can be likened to an ocean—sometimes an ocean with calm, gentle waves lapping on the shore or, at times, with huge rolling waves. The Essenes taught of the heart as "a sea with mighty waves" and of love as being "stronger than the currents of deep water."

We are love, as we are watery beings, and our true resonance is one of love. We are, each one of us, inherently one with the ocean of love, an ocean that connects us all with each other. The angel of love brings peace to the ocean. She calms the rolling surf of our emotions, bringing peace to our feelings with love.

Our heart and the heart of the earth are one heart. The water flows through the earth's rivers, as the blood flows through our veins. We can call on the angel of water as we bathe or swim to cleanse us of any challenging emotions, and the angel of water will wash them away, recycling them back to the earth.

We are here on the earth to learn about love—what love is, how love feels, and how love is expressed. A pure love is unconditional and completely accepting of another. To the

Essenes, the essence of the practise of love was compassion. This is a love that observes all beings with kind and loving eyes, because it knows that all beings suffer.

Compassion is detached and warm, wise and accepting; it is love in perfect practise. We may say the greatest journey of the soul is love.

We are learning about love. We often have notions of love as romantic love, often transient in its nature. We may compromise ourselves to receive a semblance of love, from someone who knows not how to love. This is not love but dependency, a cry from the soul for love, a cry from the child we once were for love.

The angel of love is love. She gives us complete unconditional and divine love—a love not of a usual human experience. As we heal ourselves with the angel of love, we heal those who have preceded us, including our parents. We heal our ancestors of the unlove they may have felt. We free our descendants and the generations to come of our family patterns of unlove. With the angels, we can dissolve the repetitive cycles of unlove. This is a time for a new beginning for love, when the patterns of unlove can be healed.

The Essenes knew:

> Every one that loves is born of the Divine, and knows the angels. (*The Essene Gospel of Peace*)

We learned how to love from our parents, and they learned from their parents. Our parents are our role models for love and how to express that love. We observe our parents in their giving and receiving of love. The experience of love, or unlove, as a child, is absorbed by the cells of our body, and it settles deep within our subconscious being.

If we are blessed, we are born in a family secure in its love, a family that knows how to express its love. Or it may be our parents were unable to express love or treated us unkindly. This would then create a cycle of unlove, which may have been perpetuated down the generations. The angel of love heals all of these things—anything at all which is unlove is healed. The angels do not judge, as whatever the outer casing, within each of us is the essence love. Sometimes it is close to the surface and the person is able to express and feel that love within. In others, the essence of love is buried so deeply they have yet to find its source.

Love has a transformative quality, and love is a catalyst for change. Invoke the angel of love, and she will bring healing, change, and hope for the future. The Essenes taught that, "No man is an island." The new beginning for love starts inside ourselves, and as our feelings of unlove are replaced with love, the love that we feel flows out to our family too.

Love is a gift from the angels and the Mother Earth. The earth loves us as her children, as we are her family. To the earth and the angels, we are one family of humanity. We can:

> Call on the Angel of Love to enter into our feelings, that they may be purified. And all that was before impatience and discord will turn to harmony and peace, as the parched ground drinks in the gentle rain and becomes green and soft, tender with new life. (The Essene *Gospel of Peace*)

The Essene family

The Essenes either lived a monkish life, or they lived as families. To the Essenes, the family was the core of their society. They believed that, sometimes, it is easier to love those unknown to us, than our family, because when we live with our family, they see our faults.

The Essenes believed that love, justice, and fairness were key qualities that engender a harmonious family and community. In their family lives, they had identified and put into practise four expressions of love. These were conjugal love, paternal love, filial love, and fraternal love.

Conjugal love was the love between married couples, who they considered to be the heart of the Essene home. They believed it was the couple's responsibility to maintain a warm, loving, and harmonious family home, whilst living according to the Essene principles.

Paternal love was the parents' love for their children. The Essenes were a very practical people, who endeavoured to teach by example. They believed their children would eventually teach the same qualities to their own children in the future. Important to them were care, consideration, and mutual respect between parent and child. With the spiritual life of the child in mind, when the child had reached a certain age, he or she came under the care of the most spiritually adept Essenes within their community.

Essene parents believed they had a duty of care towards their children. They believed in a reciprocal love and care between each generation.

When parents were elderly, the roles would reverse, and the children would take up their responsibility of a duty of care towards their parents. This was an expression of filial love, or the love of the child for the parent.

The fourth expression of love in the Essene family was the love between siblings, which was known as fraternal love. Love between siblings was encouraged, because the Essenes believed siblings who loved one other would support and love each other throughout their lives.

The Essenes wrote:

> Then shall Man seek peace with his own feelings,
> that his family may delight in his loving kindness,
> even his father, his mother, his wife, his children, and
> his children's children. (*The Essene Gospel of Peace*)

Forgiveness is golden

The Essenes taught of love, and they taught of forgiveness. They taught us to love the Mother Earth and the Divine but first that we must love ourselves and each other. To the Essenes, the greatest expression of love was forgiveness. It was a quality they believed humanity sorely needed, as the wounds of the past and the present run deep. Forgiveness is gift of grace from the angels, so we may free ourselves from the bitterness of the past.

Grace is a quality of the love of the Divine, which falls as an unseen spiritual rain from the heavens, as the following quotation from Shakespeare's Merchant of Venice describes: "The quality of mercy is not strained, it droppeth as the gentle rain from heaven."

Forgiveness is the gold of our soul. To the Essenes, there was nothing to forgive, as everything we experience is chosen by our soul. If we believe we chose our experiences, then it follows they must already be forgiven. We are the instruments of our souls, here to learn from the experience of love and also the experience of unlove. We chose our family, who are the characters in our soul story, because this is how we can all experience and grow in the journey of love.

For the Essenes:

When Man calls on the Angel of Love, then is the darkness dispersed. And the light of sunshine streams from him and the colours of the rainbow swirl about his head. Gentle rains fall from his fingers, and he brings peace and strength to all those who draw near to him. (The Essene *Gospel of Peace*)

The family of the light

The third day pertains to the solar plexus chakra. The word *solar* means sun, the solar plexus being our connection with our inner sun, or inner light. When in balance, this chakra creates happiness, confidence, and a sunny disposition.

The Essenes believed the sun in the sky shone, not only with light but also with love—a love that shone unconditionally on all beings. They believed this light of unconditional love was also to be found within us, as an inner sun that shines continuously and is a connection to our inner divinity.

The Essene Aramaic word for light, or sun, is *shema*, which is the root of their word for divinity, *shemaya*. To the Essenes, the sun within was the light of the Divine. They believed we each have in our centre a divine spark of light, a light that is part of our soul—a light that shines constantly and yet is unseen.

We each contain this light, this essence of love within us. The Essenes, as the children of light, believed they were carriers of this light, as we too, carry this light. It glows as a tiny, brilliant sun within us, and it is here that we connect with the angels. They wrote:

> Let your love be as the sun which shines on all the
> creatures of the Earth, and does not favour one blade
> of grass for another. (The Essene *Gospel of Peace*)

The Essenes were spiritual adepts. They were versed in the ancient mysteries and the knowledge of the light. They came out of ancient Egypt as part of the people of Judea. They were the high priests who were given the secret inner teachings. Their soul purpose as a group of people was to ground the light upon the earth.

They taught of the light and the way of love. Their teachings reverberate through the centuries in the creeds of the gnostics, the mystics, and the Cathars, those who followed the inner light.

The Cathars lived in the south of France until the thirteenth century. They were a people who believed they did not need the intermediary of the church to communicate with God, as they held the light within them, which was their connection with the Divine. They were known as the "Perfecti," as they wished to live their lives as perfectly as possible. They followed the inner path, living close to the truth and aligned with nature. They were a people who lived closely aligned to the teachings of the Essenes.

The Essenes believed we had more than one family, both of which are connected with our soul—the family we are born into, our genetic family, and our other family, which we may call our spiritual family. Our spiritual family are those who are aligned with the purpose of our soul—those with similar spiritual interests and a desire for change. To the Essenes, their spiritual family were those who "walked with the angels"—whose mission it was to spread love in the world. Sometimes the two families will become one. How this will manifest in our life depends upon our karma and what is for our highest good.

Our spiritual family may live all over the world. We may never have met in the past. But these days, we are often drawn together as a call from the soul—as a brotherhood and sisterhood of light, and our companions on the journey of the soul.

For the Essenes:

Even so shall you love your brothers by blood, as you love all your true brothers who walk with the angels. (The Essene *Gospel of Peace*)

The angel of love asks us to be like the sun, shining our light and our love in the world. The sun of the soul glows always inside, the place where the angels dwell.

He who has found peace with his brothers has entered the kingdom of love.

—*The Essene Gospel of Peace*

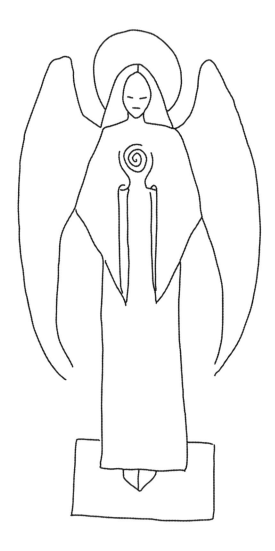

Angel of creative work

Chapter 7

Day Four, Wednesday
Angel of Creative Work

Angel invocation

> I ask the Angel of Peace to always be with me, and
> I ask the Angel of Creative Work to be with all
> of humankind, that we may receive the blessing
> of our sacred task.
>
> —*The Essene Gospel of Peace*

The gift of the angel of creative work: Peace with humanity
Heart chakra: Green

The angel on the fourth day is the angel of creative work, the gift of this angel being peace with humanity. During the first three days of the week, we invite in the angels who guide us with the personal side of our lives, our physical health and well-being and our thoughts and feelings. The angel of life gives us peace with our body, the angel of power peace with our thoughts, and the angel of love peace with our feelings and our family. The angel on the fourth day, the angel of creative work, takes us beyond the purely personal to a connection with the whole of humanity.

The angel of creative work teaches us that we are all players in a grand cosmic plan, and we each have a purpose in this plan. We have a task to fulfil. We may consider our task to be noble or humble. Whether distinguished or humble, the tasks are of equal value. This was an essential tenet of the Essenes. Everyone was equal, and everything everyone did was of equal value.

Whether we sweep the streets or are a queen on her throne, it matters not what we do. It is the energy, or the quality we put into each and every action—even those we consider insignificant—that matters. We can ask ourselves, How much love and care can I put into the small tasks, as well as the big tasks throughout my day? The humblest cleaner can express more love and care in the way he or she cleans the door handles than the loftiest person may express in his or her ruling of nations.

The angel of creative work is everywhere, whether we live in a palace or a shack. In the eyes of the angels, wherever we live, we are all equal. Whether our skin be dark or fair, we are all equal. Whether rich or poor, we are all equal:

> There are many and diverse flowers. Who shall say that one is best because its colour is purple, or that one is favoured because its stalk is long and slender? (The Essene *Gospel of Peace*)

All people and everything everyone does is equal. Whatever the colour of our skin, whichever belief system we aspire to, or whatever we do, we are all equal. The Essene mantra for society was equality and justice. This was not a justice of rulers, but a justice aligned with divine law. For the Essenes:

> In the Law of nature, all men being equal and brothers in rights, it recommends to them only peace and toleration, even for errors." (*The Essene Code of Life*)

These words were spoken by an Essene called Banus. He lived nearly two thousand years ago, and his teachings were recorded by a young Roman called Josephus Flavius, to whom Banus taught the Essene principles of life. His words are recorded in *The Essene Code of Life*, as translated by Edmond Bordeaux Szekely. To have words directly from an Essene is precious indeed. The noble mind of this man is given voice in his words.

Banus defined justice with one sentence: "Do to another the good which you would wish to receive from him." He described how, in the Essene tradition, the natural and cosmic law, which they lived by, defined justice as *equality*, *liberty*, and *property*. These are defined as:

- Equality—We are all equal because we have a body and a right to life.
- Liberty—We have a right to be free. No one has the right to dominate another. And no one should be subjected to another.
- Property—We own our body and the produce of our labour.
- Justice in alignment with divine law maintains its own equilibrium because it is founded on liberty, equality, and fairness.

In other words, freedom, fairness, and all being of equal value are all part of living according to natural and cosmic laws.

The Essenes were exemplary of these principles in their lives. They lived separately from their fellow countrymen, as they lived according to their law, the One Law. They did not live according to the rules of their country, as the perfection of their justice, the One Law, was the foundation of every aspect of their lives and livelihood:

> For we are not rich and neither are we poor and
> we share all things, even our garments and the
> tools we use to till the soil, and together we work
> in the fields with all the angels, bringing forth the

gifts of the Mother Earth for all to eat. (*The Essene
Gospel of Peace*)

On the fourth day, as we come to the heart chakra, the
teachings of Banus, the Essene, call us back to the heart. He
teaches us the natural system of justice that the Essenes lived by is
an inherent part of the One Law. It is the divine law of the natural
world in which we live. To live according to the following axioms
is to live in alignment with the creed of the One Law:

> Your father is the cosmos. Your mother is nature.
> Your brothers are your fellowmen. Live in
> harmony with the laws and forces of the universe,
> nature and your own Being. Preserve yourself.
> Learn the natural and cosmic laws. Live in peace
> with yourself, with humanity, with nature and
> the universe. Live in creative love with and for
> your fellowmen that they may live for you. (As
> spoken by Banus the Essene, from *The Essene Code
> of Life*)

The Essenes believed that to live in accordance with these
axioms was to live a life of abundance. Both excess and lack were
considered to be deviations from the law. Humanity has deviated
from living aligned with the One Law and so has had to create
hundreds of different laws to bring a semblance of justice and
of harmonious living. We have become disconnected from the
natural flow of the laws of nature. We have become disconnected
from the laws of manifestation, which state kind thoughts create
kind feelings that then manifest as kind deeds.

Love in action

There is a shift in consciousness inside us as we come to the fourth day. The angel of creative work opens our hearts to extend towards our neighbours and humanity as a whole. The hearts of humanity have been closed for a long time, as we have lived for ourselves and our own self- interests. We have believed in separation and competition, survival of the fittest. These beliefs are all born of fear. Banus teaches us to "live in creative love with and for your fellowmen."

We each have a purpose, however modest or grand, which is our soul purpose. While each individual's soul purpose may be different, all are equal in their value. The angel of creative work is the key to finding our creative self-expression and our creative purpose. This angel teaches us that, although we are all so different, each one of us has a soul purpose. When we find our soul purpose, we have reached a level of spiritual development where we know that we are all of equal value, and everything we do is of equal value. Our soul purpose was chosen by our soul, so how could it be anything but the most perfect expression of our soul. When we come to this realisation, we recognise there is no such thing as competition. We are all working together to create beauty and harmony in our own unique and individual way:

> The Angel of Creative Work sings in the humming of the bee, pausing not in its making of golden honey, in the flute of the shepherd, who sleeps not lest his flock goes astray, in the song of the maiden as she lays her hand to the spindle. And if you think that these are not as fair in the eyes of the Divine as the loftiest of prayers echoed from the highest mountain, then you do indeed err.
> (*The Essene Gospel of Peace*)

The angel of creative work teaches us the most important ingredient in our actions is the energy or the love we put into them. Our thoughts and our feelings come together in what we do. Before we can act, we first have to have a thought. Our thoughts will then flow into our feelings, which then will manifest as our actions.

Key to the Essene understanding of human nature was the relationship between our thoughts, our feelings, and our actions. Our body is designed for action—to move, to create. We can be creative in each and every moment. Creativity is not reserved only for artists or writers. Creativity is our unique expression of who we are in each moment. Our daily work, and each small task within the day, has the potential to be an expression of our creative self. With the guidance of the Angel of creative work, our relationship with our work and our actions will change. We begin to see each action we make as an opportunity to express something uniquely of ourselves, as an expression of our heart.

Our thoughts and feelings are intrinsically intertwined with our physical bodies. They operate as a trine, each dependent upon one the other. We need all three to be in balance to become the creative being we have the potential to be. We need heart to give voice to our thoughts. We need a body to express what we think and feel in our actions. How do we express our love other than through our words or our actions?

The angel of creative work is the strongest of the angels of the Divine, because it is in our actions that we can manifest the dreams of our thoughts and express the passion of our feelings. The work that we do with our body is usually with our hands. Our hands are an expression of our heart chakra. They each have a small chakra located in the centre of the palm, which is a connection with our heart chakra. It is through our hands that we may express the love we feel in our heart in our actions.

We all may have experienced how food from a loving home, cooked by loving hands tastes better. The ingredients may be the same, but the one magic ingredient is the love and care that have gone into the preparation of the food. We may even express our love in the way in which we wash the dishes after the meal.

The angel of creative work encourages us to enjoy the humble tasks in life. This is the secret to happiness—to find happiness in all of the ordinary moments in life.

The gift of service

We see the state of the world around us—the poverty, unfairness, and destruction, and we feel overwhelmed and powerless. The angel of work is an angel of creative empowerment. He shows each one of us how we may contribute and make a difference. Change begins in the little things. The big things can seem overwhelming, but if we focus our attention on the little things in life, we are empowered and enabled. As we put our love in the little things, this energy will then flow to the big things, and positive change can happen. This is a universal law.

Work is love in action, and the work we are to do is always in relation to our karma and our dharma. From an Essene perspective, the law of karma is "the foresight of the effects and consequences of our actions." We cannot change our karma; it is as it is. What we can do is sow positive seeds for a positive karma. This is called dharma.

Karma and dharma are cosmic laws aligned with the One Law. Every one of us lives by these two laws. Whether we are conscious of this or not, the laws of karma and dharma are always in motion. We may feel this is an overbearing law, but in truth, it is the opposite. They are laws of balance and equilibrium. Nature must always find its balance, and we are part of nature. The law of dharma embraces opportunity. To align ourselves with the law of dharma is to find our soul purpose in this life.

We each have a unique gift to offer to others. We may or may not know what this may be in the present time, but this gift is a seed, dormant and expectant with vast opportunities. The gift that is waiting to be unwrapped is that of finding our service to the world. It's the gift of finding out what the unique contribution we can make to create a positive difference is. The angel of creative work opens our heart so we may discover how we may be of service to the world and discover what our sacred task is. This is the gift that will make your heart sing. It is the work your soul would love to do. This is a gift of the angel of creative work:

> For the strongest of the angels, the Angel of Creative Work, blesses each person who works in the way best for him, for then shall he know neither want nor excess. Truly is there abundance for all … when each works at his task. (*The Essene Gospel of Peace*)

The key to spiritual abundance lies in unwrapping this gift. We tend to value the work we do in terms of how much money we earn in an hour, a day, or a year. This is a mindset born of materialism, which creates a disconnection from our heart. A creative consciousness shift is awaiting humanity—from how much money we can earn in each unit of time to how much love and care we can put into whatever we are doing in the same unit of time. Time becomes an art form, as opposed to a currency. A natural abundance will then flow, as this is a secret of the overflowing heart—a heart that gives with love and receives with love. When we are doing what we love to do is when we lose track of time. We feel joy in whatever we are doing, however large or small the task.

The change in our attitude to what we call work begins with our attention to detail. Do we do whatever we are doing with love and care? Do we put love into how we open the door handle or sweep the floor? The beginning of the consciousness shift is this simple; it is expressing our love and care in the little things in life. It takes practise, but eventually even the simplest and humblest of tasks gives us pleasure, and all because the task, whatever it may be, is valued and we care.

This quality of mindfulness then emanates into the big things in life, such as important decisions to be made in careers, home, or relationships. The practise begins in the little things, and then the big things will take care of themselves. As we practise putting the love in the little things, we open ourselves to receive a spiritual flow of abundance. Our cup is no longer empty, or half full; it is overflowing. This is the gift of the angel of creative work. The wheel of dharma turns, and we are at the centre, receiving absolute abundance, aligned with the cosmic law of natural order, the One Law.

Conscious community

We are pioneers of a brave new world, and what we need to maintain its balance is heart. We have the internet and a potentially instant connection with anyone upon the planet. Our relationships have changed from immediate to extensive. We can communicate with many people at one time, via social media, websites, and emails.

Whilst this may seem the antithesis of peace, it is part of the plan of peace. The invisible grid of communication is akin to an electronic collective unconscious—a place where we are all equal and we each have a voice. The extent of our care and concern for others expands, as we are privy to their worlds.

It is very easy to become discouraged by the negativity we can see in the media. We may feel helpless and disempowered, but there is a solution. The Essene intention was to always strengthen the light, to focus on the positive. Darkness is purely lack of light;

if we fill a space with light, the darkness will disappear. We see this every morning in nature when the sun rises.

Our minds are powerful, and intention is our greatest tool. Whatever we focus on is what will grow. If we focus on the positive, then it will grow. We must focus on the solution and not on the problem. An empowering adage is to focus on the little things, and the big things will look after themselves.

Within the collective of humanity, each one of us is unique, and each of us has a contribution we can make to the greater good. The angel of creative Work is the stepping stone from our little individual world to the greater world of humanity. This angel knows the role we have to play in the divine plan for humanity and the earth—gently encouraging us to let go of our individual, egoistic will and say *yes* to being aligned with the higher will, so we may be part of creating the new earth.

This is a new beginning for humanity. The Angel of creative work teaches us to trust in the big plan—to know everything that happens is in alignment with this plan and divine pattern and order.

It can only be so, as we live within the laws of creation. Imbalances will always rebalance; nature will always maintain its own equilibrium. The angels ask us to be joyful and to trust. We are all equal in the eyes of the angels, and each one of us has a unique gift to offer to humanity and the earth. It is all part of the divine plan.

Within our world of expanding networks, community is key to the new consciousness. We are one community of human beings living upon the Mother Earth. We are one community with all of the other creatures who live on her surface, and we are completely interdependent, one with the other.

As we open our hearts, the angel of creative work gives us the gift of love and compassion for all. We have believed we are separate from those of a different colour skin, from those who have other beliefs. We are all one; we are one family of humanity.

The atoms of our cells are all aligned with the same One Law. The angels teach us this, and the Essenes lived by this. To receive the gift of our sacred task is a gift from the angels to each one of us from all corners of the globe, as unique individuals with a positive contribution to offer.

We each have our own truth, we each have our own way, and we each have our own unique consciousness to share with one another. Shine your own light, follow your own path, and put your love into whatever you do.

> Those who have found peace with the brotherhood of Man have made them self a co-worker with the Divine.
>
> —*The Essene Gospel of Peace*

Angel of wisdom

Chapter 8

Day Five, Thursday
Angel of Wisdom

Angel invocation

> I ask the Angel of Peace to always be with me,
> and I ask the Angel of Wisdom to guide my
> knowledge, that I may walk in the paths of the
> great ones who have seen the face of the Divine.
> —*The Essene Gospel of Peace*

The gift of the angel of wisdom: Peace with culture
Throat chakra: Blue

On the fifth day, we climb the mountain to the throat chakra. The air is rarefied high in the mountains; it is not where we are used to living. We are closer to the Divine and closer to the angels. In Sanskrit, the word for the throat chakra is *vishuddha*, which means purified.

We can consider the invocation of the angel of power, on the second day, as being a prelude to the angel of wisdom on the fifth day. We invoked the angel of power so we may think peaceful thoughts, that we may be more aware of the power of our thoughts and use them wisely. On the second day, our sacral chakra is purified as we heal the genetic patterns we have inherited from our ancestors. The flowering of the purification of the sacral chakra occurs at the throat chakra. When we are operating from the throat chakra, we become an open channel for divine inspiration to flow through us. As divine inspiration flows through us, we may think divine thoughts, which inspire divine feelings and create divine actions.

At the level of the throat chakra we have reached the non-personal sphere. During the first three days of the week, the angels guide us in the personal side of our life—our bodies, our thoughts, and our feelings. On the fourth day, the angel of creative work leads us to embrace our fellow human beings. On the fifth day, we climb the mountains and touch the realm of the angels and the Divine.

The throat chakra may feel as if it is an empty space. We have left the green of the heart and nature and are now in the blue of emptiness—a place of absolute trust, because the world of form and boundaries has dissolved. To relate from the purified space of the throat chakra is a place unfamiliar to most. The air is thin in the mountains; it is a long and arduous climb to the top. For the Essenes:

> Beyond the icy peaks of struggle, lies the peace
> and beauty of the Infinite Garden of Knowledge,
> where the meaning of the Law is made known to
> the children of light. (*The Essene Gospel of Peace*)

To view the world from the mountain peaks comes at the price of the inner transformation, which happens as we take responsibility for our thoughts and feelings. Most people are identified in the three lower chakras—the root, the sacral, and the solar plexus. Their reality is entrenched in the world of making ends meet, doing what you do not love to do, competition, wanting more and more, or not having enough to supply life's basic needs. All of these, whether excess or want, are expressions of living out of alignment with the One Law.

To find peace at the throat chakra is to completely trust the process of life. We may think of the angels of the Essenes as our guardians or guides. Maybe we can imagine them invisibly holding our hands with their wingtips, guiding us each step of the way as loving, non-judgemental companions.

As we purify our thoughts and feelings, with the angels, we come to vishhuddha, our purified state. This is where we emerge from the chrysalis of transformation into the butterfly. The sacral chakra is the seat of our personal creative powers. The throat chakra is where our creativity makes a transdimensional shift from personal to spiritual. A gateway opens to divine inspiration, and we become a conduit for a divine flow of energy to flow through us.

This is a gift from the angels, to take our rightful place as a cocreator with the angels and as a cocreator with the Divine. This is all part of the divine plan for our soul. When we reach this place of peace and trust, we are the artists of our own life and destiny. We have surrendered to the divine process of life and found the ultimate peace.

For the Essenes:

> It was for this that you have waited seven years to learn how to speak to the angels, for you know not the power of your thoughts. Use then, wisdom in all you think and say and do. (*The Essene Gospel of Peace*)

The ancient scrolls

The Essenes laid great store by studying their ancient texts, which were their priceless inheritance. Their texts were a light of truth lit centuries before, even before the time of Enoch, their great forefather. They considered those who wrote the ancient texts as having seen the face of the Divine and those who read the texts as touching the feet of the Divine.

> "For it was said of old, that in the beginning there were giants in the earth, and mighty men of renown. And the children of light shall guard and preserve their written word. Lest we become again as beasts, and know not the kingdom of the angels. (*The Essene Gospel of Peace*)

The Essene mode of learning was holistic. It was an education of the head, heart, and body. Aligned with their philosophy of "the body, the heart and the mind as one." Their learning process was a merging of the mind, with a feeling experience in the heart and an integration of the two in the body.

It differs greatly from our modern education regime, where the mind is king. The whole of life was their teacher, "through the light of the mind, through the light of nature, and through the study of the sacred word."

The light of nature is the living book of nature, which speaks to our heart. This is a teaching we observe and feel. The laws of nature are everywhere around us and teach, through their reflections, the living One Law. When teaching, the Essenes preferred to speak from parables in nature, as the symbology was easily understood by the masses.

There are layers upon layers within the teachings of the Essenes. We can travel to the depths of the oceans and the heights of the mountains on their words. The words will settle in our hearts', dependent upon our receptivity. The living book of nature is the unwritten law—a Law of many depths for those with the eyes to see and the ears to hear the voice of Mother Earth.

The written law speaks to our mind. The written law is found within the ancient texts the Essenes inherited from their ancestors—the great teachers who had "seen the face of the

Divine." These texts were part of their trinity of wisdom and an essential part of their learning. To understand the teachings in the ancient texts, the written law was prerequisite to understanding the unwritten Law of Nature.

> The written Law is the instrument by which the unwritten Law is understood, as the mute branch of a tree becomes a singing flute in the hands of the shepherd. (*The Essene Gospel of Peace*)

The completion of their trinity of wisdom was that of gnosis, the experience of an inner knowing, which is unique for each individual. Gnosis is the path of the mystic and the intuition; it is the gold of wisdom. It is where knowing about something becomes an inner knowing. The body, the heart, and the mind have come together as one, which opens the door to the inner knowing. This is where we become the flute that sings the song of the Divine and the songs of the angels. To the Essene, this was the holy grail of wisdom.

To attain gnosis is to open the pages of the eternal book of the soul. This book of the soul is our inner teacher, who is revealed as we bring our body, mind, and heart together as one. All we need to know is already within us, but we have forgotten this, which is the heritage of our soul. We are each a master in waiting, who is looking for the pot of gold at the end of the rainbow—the pot of gold of our spiritual abundance. To chase the rainbow is illusionary. We will never arrive, as it moves as we move, a little like a carrot on the end of a stick. Our own pot of gold, the gold of gnosis, lies within us. When we find this is when we can open the pages of the eternal book of our soul, a book that is inside each one of us.

The Essene description of gnosis was the opening of the sacred scroll. To read the sacred scroll was the realm of the great masters and teachers of the Essenes, those who had climbed the highest of the mountains. They were the ones who wrote the ancient texts for us to read. Their words are often poetic and rhythmic in their nature, their intonation a reflection of divine pattern and order. Gnosis is the gold of wisdom. For the Essenes:

> The Angel of Wisdom ... makes Man free from fear, wide of heart and easy of conscience. Sacred wisdom, the understanding that unfolds continuously as a sacred scroll, yet does not come through learning. (*The Essene Gospel of Peace*)

Wisdom is all

There is a difference between knowledge and wisdom. Knowledge is acquired when we learn about something; wisdom is gained with experience. When we read a text, we have gained knowledge. When we have integrated that knowledge inside ourselves, when it has become second nature to us, it becomes wisdom. Wisdom is a quality that comes with experience, and often with age.

In Western culture, we have lost touch with the wisdom of the elders—those with a depth of wisdom, unlearned but born of life's experiences. We all have a genetic wisdom from our family lineage, which is encoded within our DNA. But we have lost touch with this too. In the far distant past, we all lived innately connected with the wisdom of the Earth and nature. This is now only remembered by those from indigenous cultures. But the many branches of our family trees all stem from one source, deep in the trunk that roots itself within the earth herself.

We do not learn wisdom at school. The modern style of schooling is focused on educating the mind. We are graded according to our comprehension and retention of information. The angel of wisdom teaches us to value not only our mind, but also our heartfelt knowing and our intuition. For these, and not the education of the mind alone, are the three paths to a true knowledge and inner wisdom. To manifest our potential as human beings is to use the power of our mind, the feeling knowing of our heart, and our intuition unified together as one.

A secret of the angel of wisdom is the star within. The star is part of our subtle anatomy not known of by many. The star is where we hear the whisperings of our soul. It is our connection to the inner sacred scrolls so highly revered by the Essenes. The star is a very bright point of light, which sits inside the centre of our body, a little way above the navel and a little way inside the body. This very tiny and bright star is part of our true aura; it is a walnut-sized energy package that contains the potential of our soul.

The star is one of the biggest secrets of the angels. If we listen to the teaching of the Essenes it is our key to connecting with the angels, as it is in "the centre where the angels of day and of night mingle." The star and the angels are our pot of gold at the end of the rainbow. The beauty and perfection of creation is within, and each of us is a grail that contains this perfection and beauty. We do not need to journey far to find this beauty, because the beauty and the wisdom we seek is within:

> When the Angel of Wisdom governs your deeds, then is the path to the unknown realms established, and order and harmony govern your lives. (*The Essene Gospel of Peace*)

The living truth

Throughout the ages, there have been many great spiritual teachers. There are those who have taught great teachings of the mind. Others have taught how to love with the heart. And some traditions have taught us to honour and revere the body. Many of the ancient teachings have been sullied by man, but there is an essence of truth that lies within all.

The Essene truth was a living relationship with truth. Their truth was not static, but dynamic and changing. As they journeyed with the angels, they transformed and grew. Their daily angel meditations were their means of transformation, as they journeyed to become one with the great creative mind—to become a cocreator with the Divine.

Truth can be subjective, until we come to a point of spiritual development when it becomes a more objective truth. Truth needs to be balanced with love. The truth of the mind has limitations; the truth of the heart may be illusionary. The big *truth* of our destination is when we balance the truth of the mind with the truth of our heart as one truth. The angels empower us to follow the path of our own truth. My truth may differ from your truth. There are many paths up the mountain to the one truth.

The angel of creative work teaches us love, justice, and tolerance. We are taught we are all equal in the eyes of the divine. All the while we think we are separate, we see humanity as fractured into seemingly complex fragments of identity. The angels teach us we are all one, and our belief in our separation is an illusion. We purely journey on different paths up the mountain that is called truth. We can see farther from the mountaintops. A new horizon is visible to us. Cities and towns are seen in one field of vision. The distances that separate people are less.

When we fly in a plane, we cross many borders. We can sense the presence of the thousands of people who live below. Humanity has created a patchwork quilt on the surface of the earth. Not only are there the picturesque patterns of fields and forest, but there also exists a pattern of an abundance of belief systems, cultures, and religions, which are expressed visibly as beautiful religious buildings or sacred spaces or invisibly as thought forms of belief, which touch the heart with their truth. We are rich with the teachings from the past, and we are not separate, because we simply journey on our own path toward the top of the mountain.

The angel of wisdom teaches us wisdom and tolerance, opening our heads and our hearts to both truth and love. We are all individual and unique with a richness to offer to others. To walk high in the mountains with the angels is to perceive and feel the richness of that diversity. We all have our own truth, and each one of us is a drop of truth in the ocean of planetary consciousness. We are each one drop in the ocean of human collective consciousness, and we are all unique in our individuality. As the paths merge closer towards the top of the mountain, a new consciousness of acceptance and tolerance is possible—one of wisdom and openness, sharing and learning, the beginnings of peace with culture.

The breath of peace

They say the angels like high places. Above the clouds in the pure blue sky, we are closer to the Divine. To the Essenes, the blue sky was the symbol for a peaceful mind. In the Buddhist tradition this is *dharmakaya*, the unity of all things, manifest and unmanifest, the absolute peace that is possible.

Peace is silence, and yet peace is found in movement also. We have the potential to feel peaceful in every moment, if we can become conscious of how we breathe. Our breath flows in and out of our body for our whole life. But we are not conscious of our breath, any more than we are conscious of how our thoughts and feelings may affect others. The ancient Essenes had the possibility of feeling peaceful in each moment, through an awareness of the breath.

A gift of the angel of wisdom is the gift of peaceful, relaxed breathing. The breath flows deep inside the body with this angel, to the star in the belly. Allow your belly to relax and flow with the breath—gently expanding on the in breath and falling on the out breath, relaxing all of the muscles and the organs. Most importantly, let go on the out breath of any tensions in the body, for this is a key to peace. We may let go of any troubling thoughts, feelings, or tensions in the body on the out breath.

To be present with our breath is to be present with spirit— the invisible spirit that pervades all things. To the Essenes, the breath was the divine itself. My breath, your breath, our breath, is the breath of the divine spirit that flows around the Earth. All breath is sacred and is the breath of the Divine, and to breathe consciously is to breathe in rhythm with nature itself.

In the words of the Essenes:

> Angel of Air, sacred messenger of the Mother Earth, enter deep within me, as the swallow plummets from the sky, that I may know the secrets of the wind and the music of the stars. (*The Essene Gospel of Peace*)

Just for a moment, we can visualise ourselves standing high on a mountain and looking at a lake below, where the air is clear and blue, with not a cloud in the sky, and the sky is perfectly reflected in the lake below. The Essenes believed the pale blue sky was the perfect peace of the Divine, and this was then reflected in the water below. This is perfect example of the One Law—as above, so below. The pale blue sky is the divine blueprint. It is the most perfect peace possible, and it is also the breath—the most sacred of the elements to the Essenes. The breath is our doorway to peace. The angels teach us our purpose is to create peace and become the peace we wish to see in the world. So we can share the light of peace of the angels with others.

Sound and silence

Peace is a mystery. It is a living, divine truth—a divine template for creation. Our essential nature is peace; this is our own truth. The essence of our vibration is one of peace, but it has only been hidden under layers of conditioned patterns of stress and tension.

Peace is found in silence and also in sound. Both are vibrational, although sound is more active and silence passive. The whole of the universe is vibration of differing resonances. The intoning of sacred sound and sacred names were part of the Essene tradition. As cocreators with the angels, the Essenes believed that to speak the names of the angels was a powerful spiritual practise. Sound is vibration, and to invoke an angel by its name is to activate powerful healing frequencies that we may feel as vibrations in our body. These vibrations heal our cellular structure and our DNA. They purify our emotions and clear our thoughts. The vibration of sound also penetrates our aura, filling it with the energy of light.

When we practise the angel meditations and invoke the angel by name, we may feel the vibration of the angel's name resonating in our aura and body as a tingle or flow of energy. We connect with the angels through our feelings. We may know about them in our mind, but our experience of angelic energy is one of feeling. With practise, we may even be able to identify each angel's specific calling card, through the vibrational quality we feel in our body, as the vibration of each of the angels is unique. Until adept at this practise, it is easier to feel their vibration while quiet or silent, especially during the angel meditation. But with practise our sensitivity grows and we become sensitive to their energies at other times too.

To enhance our ability to sense the vibrational quality of the angels, it can be helpful to practise a "feeling listening." This is not a feeling listening with our ears but with the whole of our body. Our entire thinking-feeling-body continuum becomes an angel antenna, and with practise, the angelic energies will gradually become more tangible. The angels become part of our living, feeling experience.

It is important we make time to be silent, to be in a quiet space. It is then easier to be receptive to the world of subtle vibrations. The art of meditation and silence enhance our sensitivity and receptivity. When we initially start to meditate, we may feel we need absolute quiet to do so. But with practise, we find we can meditate effectively even with a small degree of noise in the background, which can be helpful in our modern way of life. Peace is possible in all situations and in all places, because the angels are everywhere around us and at all times.

As we practise peace, it grows. The key is not to try to make peace happen but to relax and let go into peace. Peace begins as inner peace. We can create for ourselves a sanctuary of peace, our own sacred space in which to practise our meditation with the angels. As we meditate in our chosen space, the energy of peace will grow. Peace will grow inside us and around us, as we create an energy field of peace during our meditation. As our peace grows, we will carry the energy of peace with us wherever we go. We will share peace with others simply by being more peaceful. By being present with others in our peacefulness, we will share the energy of peace, as an unseen gift from ourselves and the angels. We are empowered by the angels to create peace by being peace.

The art of creating sacred space is well known in some traditions, especially those of Asia. It is sometimes possible to happen across a temple in the busiest of cities, and find an atmosphere imbued with peace and calm. This is an example of the power of intention, and the prayers and meditations of those who care for the space and visit it. We can create our own sacred space for the angel meditations in a corner of our home or, even better, outside in nature, maybe close to a tree. Whether a corner of a room or a sacred temple, we can all create a sacred space to practise peace with the angels.

> He who has found peace with the teachings of the ancients ... ... has entered the cloud-filled hall of the ancients, where dwells the Sacred Brotherhood, of whom no man may speak.
>
> —*The Essene Gospel of Peace*

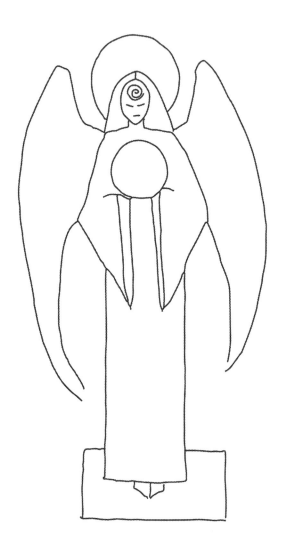

Angel of joy

Chapter 9

Day Six, Friday
Angel of Joy

Angel invocation

> I ask the Angel of Peace to always be with me,
> and I ask the Angel of Joy to be present upon
> the Mother Earth, that our hearts may be full of
> singing and gladness as we nestle in the arms of
> our Mother.
>
> —*The Essene Gospel of Peace*

The gift of the angel of joy: Peace with the Mother Earth
Brow chakra: Royal Blue

The angel on the sixth day is the angel of joy. This angel gifts us with the happiness that is possible when we live in harmony with the Mother Earth.

The Essenes believed the whole of the earth to be a garden, and in the centre of the garden is humankind. They believed themselves to be caretakers of the planet, the custodians of the living, breathing Gaia. They created a garden in the desert, in a place devoid of sufficient rain or topsoil, and all this because they worked cocreatively with the angels. To the Essenes, they were one with nature and not separate. They believed the rain, the creeks, and the oceans were the blood of the Mother Earth. The wind was her breath, and the rocks her bones, the fruit and nuts her flesh and her gift to us.

To them:

> You are one with the Mother Earth, she is in you
> and you in her ... Your breath is her breath, your
> blood her blood, your bone her bone, your eyes
> and ears are her eyes and ears. (*The Essene Gospel
> of Peace*)

The angels of nature are her angels—the angel of the sun, the angel of air, the angel of the earth, and the angel of water. These giant angels overlight the whole of the earth and the four elements that make up the earth and ourselves. Our bodies are made of the same four elements—earth, air, water, and light.

We are one with the earth, but humanity has forgotten this, especially modern man. We tend to think of the earth as an object. We mine and take her resources without thinking. We pollute the water and destroy the forests. We destroy the ecosystems that are the homes of other sentient beings. We have pushed away our mother, the earth, in pursuit of greed.

We have forgotten that we are one with the earth. Whatever happens to the earth will happen to us too. The rivers and oceans of the earth are her watery circulatory system, which is a reflection of our own circulatory system. If we pollute the rivers and oceans of the earth, which are her blood, we pollute our own blood. The blood in our body is comprised of the same water that flows in the oceans and rivers of the planet.

The air that flows around the planet is her breath. If we pollute the air of the earth, we pollute her breath and also our own breath. If we contaminate the topsoil of the earth with chemicals, we poison not only the soil, but also the food we eat. Nature is an extension of ourselves. We are not separate. We are one and the same, just expressed in different forms. We are completely codependent upon the planet, and she on us.

The prophecies of the Essenes point to this time, when

humanity and the earth are at a critical point in their evolution. They knew there would come a time when humanity would become divorced from living in unity with the Mother Earth.

> There will come a day when Man will turn his face from his Mother Earth, and betray her, even denying his Mother and his birthright. Then shall he sell her into slavery, and her flesh shall be ravaged, her blood polluted and her breath smothered. (*The Essene Gospel of Peace*)

We live inside our homes divorced from the world of nature around us, often engrossed in our technology and eating food out of packages. We commonly buy the food we eat from artificially illuminated supermarkets, where the majority of the aisles contain food that is processed in some form or another. There is an abundance of chemicals, plastics, and cans, which all require disposing of. These containers were initially manufactured from mined materials or crude oil from deep underneath the ocean floor. We take without thinking and often dispose of without thinking too.

To act with without thought or care for the earth and the other sentient beings upon her surface is to create a catastrophe of calamitous proportions. Nature will always find a balance; it is a natural process of equilibrium and is a form of healing for the earth. Extreme weather patterns are symptoms of the earth trying to maintain her natural balance, whilst being subjected to the pollution and destruction caused by the ignorance of humankind.

The Mother Earth

As a living, conscious being, the earth loves each one of unconditionally. She is unconditional in her acceptance of us even recognises each one of us as we walk upon her surface

each have an inherent energetic connection point with the Mother Earth. This is a tiny point of light called the earth star, which is found just underneath the soles of our feet, a few centimetres below the surface of the earth. As we move, our earth star moves with us, as it is part of our auric field and chakra system.

The Mother Earth recognises each one of us through our earth star. This contains all the information about who we are and where we are destined to be upon the planet. The earth observes each one of us as we move around her surface through our earth star. This energy point contains the karmic information about our relationship with the earth and why we are where we are upon the planet at any moment in time.

More than seven billion people, and their earth stars have been destined to incarnate upon the planet in this time of great awakening.

A call to the heart

This is a time many ancient prophecies have pointed to. The call to awaken comes from the earth herself. Her resurgent life force will stimulate our earth star, and the energy from the earth star will flow into our body and up to our heart. The seeds of the awakening and our new beginning create a flowering in the heart, and a new consciousness is born. There is the possibility of a rebirth in our relationship with the earth and the other sentient beings who live upon her surface.

As a species, we have lived through dark times. But we can begin to turn the corner and see the light at the end of the tunnel. It is as though we are still in midwinter, with the first snowdrops beginning to blossom, delicate points of hope in the wintery vista. The angels teach us that now is the time to return to the bosom of our Mother Earth. They teach us that, to live in union with the Mother Earth and her angels is our natural and rightful place.

Then we can learn, once again, how we may live in alignment with the One Law. This is not a law as we know it. This law was not created by humankind. It is a law of creation and is the law by which the angels live. All life on earth is created according to this one law of beauty and harmony.

The One Law is the law of nature. When we open our hearts, we can see this law in all its simplicity. If we look at a tree, we can see it always grows towards the sun, towards the light, and its roots always travel deep within the earth. Rain will always fall from above to below, and the rivers always flow from the mountains to the oceans. These are simple examples of the One Law. This is the living book of nature, the sacred book of nature of the Essenes. To live according to the One Law is the key to our own health and longevity; it is the key to peace.

The Essenes considered all illness was due to living out of alignment with the earth and the One Law. If we live as though separate from the Earth, if we believe we can take without consequence or without honouring the earth, we are living outside of the Law. It follows that we will then live in a state of disharmony, with the potential for ill health and disease.

For the Essenes:

> In everything that is life is the Law written. It is written in the grass, in the trees, in rivers, mountains, birds of the sky and fishes of the sea, and most of all within Man. (*The Essene Gospel of Peace*)

The angel of joy shows us how we may live in harmony with the earth and the one unifying law. To the ancients, to live in harmony with the law created abundant health, vitality, and longevity. All their needs were met, and there was plentiful food for all, because they were working and living with nature and not against it.

A reciprocal relationship of care, love, and respect can be fostered between ourselves and the Mother Earth. She is completely unconditional in her acceptance of us; her love is boundless. She will hold open the pages of the living book of nature for us to read, so we may step lightly upon her surface as we walk with our newfound awareness:

> The Book of Nature is a sacred scroll. If you would have humanity save themselves ... teach them, once again, to read from the living pages of the Mother Earth. (*The Essene Gospel of Peace*)

To the Essenes, the perfect life was to be a gardener, working closely with the Mother Earth and her angels in conscious co-creation. They not only believed in angels. But they also believed in nature spirits. These are the spirits of the plants and the trees, often known as devas. Unseen and unrecognised by modern man, they are sometimes perceived as coloured lights in the vicinity of the plants. Each tree and plant has its own accompanying deva and a unique consciousness of its own. Where the angels are vast cosmic beings, the devas and nature spirits are earth beings. They are the energetic gardeners of nature, and they too are conscious beings. A gift of the angel of joy is to help us to remember our place as cocreators with both the visible and the invisible worlds of nature—so we may fulfil our destiny and work as a team with the earth, her angels, and the devas.

Peace and the divine feminine

The angel of joy is the angel of the sixth chakra, the brow chakra. Another angel associated with this chakra is the angel of peace. This is the angel that is invoked on each of the seven days of the week, as a prelude to each of the angel meditations. The angel of peace is one of the angels of the Divine, and the angel of joy is one of the angels of the Mother Earth. To the Essenes, the Angel of peace was the most revered of all the angels. The peace this angel gifts us with is an otherworldly peace; it is a peace not often experienced in life. The angel of peace opens a doorway to eternity and gives us an experience of the "peace which passes understanding." This level of peace is that of the masters and the great world teachers who have lived over the centuries, those who taught about peace and also love.

In the world of the Essenes, those who had attained this level of peace had metaphorically climbed the highest mountains. To work on ourselves, to take responsibility for our thoughts and our feelings, is to climb the hills. To climb the mountains is to achieve the highest levels of spiritual awareness. The angel of joy is our guide as we climb the path to the top of the hills, with the vision of the mountains in the distance.

To touch the mountains is to experience the finest quintessence of love—a love that is expressed in its fullness by few human beings; it is the realm of the angels and the great world teachers. This quintessence of love is the love the Mother Earth has for each one of us, the love of the divine feminine.

To feel and accept unconditional love can be a process for us, as for most people, their experience of love is within personal relationships. The Mother Earth loves each and every one of us totally unconditionally, and to feel this love from our Mother Earth can be a heart-opening experience, often accompanied by tears. The love of the Mother Earth will create transformation and healing for us.

To feel the peace and joy of the angels on the sixth day is to touch our own divinity. It is our doorway to understanding the mysteries of life. The Essene initiates believed all life is the love of the Divine made manifest, and the Mother Earth is an expression of that love. She is the divine feminine, whom some may call the goddess.

To speak of a law sounds incredibly serious, but the law the Essenes lived by was the law of nature, the One Law. It was a completely different concept of law, not related to the thousands of laws humanity has made over the centuries. As humankind has deviated from the One Law of nature, people have needed to redress the imbalance by creating many of their own laws. This has manifested as a semblance of living in peace and harmony, fraught with disequilibrium and injustice. It is a system designed to fail, as it takes no account of nature as a living organism, which will always attempt to redress imbalance.

To live in alignment with the One Law of nature is a place of joy, where everything is in perfect and divine order. The homeostatic organism of the earth is complete, each part balancing the whole. We live on a thin, green film on the surface of the Earth, which we call the biosphere. It is fragile and dynamic in its complexity and beauty, and is always ruled by the laws of nature.

The sounds of nature

All of life is vibration and every life form, even the flowers, the plants and trees, have their own unique vibration and even their own sound. Nature has its own voice, but we have forgotten how to hear this voice, because our ears have become closed to the more subtle sounds of nature. These are sounds that are so soft they are almost imperceptible. When we do hear them, they are sounds we not only hear, but also feel as a vibration in our heart.

The angel of joy helps to open our brow chakra and our intuition, so we may see, hear, and feel the world of nature in astonishing ways. To open the brow chakra is to expand the senses. We may see what we had not previously seen and hear what we had not previously heard. We become attuned to the finest vibrations of nature.

Our sense of touch will be heightened to the subtle energies that surround living beings. Our sense of smell becomes attuned to the finest nuances of fragrance, an awakening of our soul to ancient memories. These are the higher mind functions. These are gifts from the angels as we open our brow chakra, so we may clearly perceive the richness around us. Humanity has been blind and deaf to the invisible realm of nature, but now we may enjoy our reconnection with this wondrous world—a remembrance for our soul, our heart, and our senses.

The angel of joy brings a celebration of life. This angel asks us to live our life lightfully and to let the seriousness dissolve. The angel invites us to open our hearts to the realm of the living book of nature, with its angels and devas—a real-life fairy story waiting to be revealed, where sometimes just a glimpse is all we require to encourage us forward.

If we can find it within ourselves to open our eyes and to live in oneness with nature, we will flourish. We all have a role to play in caring for the Mother Earth and all of the other sentient beings who live here too. The Earth is a living organism that is one giant community, and we are part of this community, which includes all of the animals and plants and even the soil, water, and air. All of the members of earth's community are codependent upon one another, as all aspects of life are interconnected. The angels ask us to take up our role as guardians of this community and as cocreators with all of the beings, both seen and unseen, who live within the realm of the Mother Earth. Then we may create peace and live in harmony with each other and live as one with the laws of nature.

> The book of nature is a sacred scroll. If you would have Man save themselves … teach them how, once again, to read from the living pages of the Mother Earth.
>
> —*The Essene Gospel of Peace*

Angel of eternal life

Chapter 10

Day Seven, Saturday
Angel of Eternal Life

Angel invocation

> I ask the Angel of Peace to always be with me,
> and I invoke the Angel of Eternal Life, that I may
> soar beyond the stars and live forever.
> —*The Essene Gospel of Peace*

The gift of the angel of eternal life: Peace with the Divine
Crown chakra: Violet

The angel on the seventh day is the angel of eternal life, who
gifts us with peace with the Divine and also peace with our own
divinity.

The Essenes believed all life on earth to be a reflection of the
divine above. This is the expression of the One Law—as above,
so below. To be sentient of the One Law and to live in alignment
with this law is to live in peace, harmony, unity, and oneness.
To the Essenes the divine was found in all the minutiae of life,
even the smallest grain of sand. This wondrous world of living
reflections was the reality of the mystical Essene. The angel of
eternal life is the angel who reveals to us the mystery of life—the
unknowable and the unseen, the hand of the Divine, which is
hidden in every leaf.

For the Essenes:

> The whole of the kingdom of the Divine may
> be found in the smallest drop of dew on a wild
> flower, or in the scent of newly cut grass in the
> field under the summer sun. (The Essene *Gospel*
> *of Peace*)

The seventh day was the Essene Sabbath—a day when they fasted until evening and rested from their work in the gardens. This was the day when they would often entertain visitors with music and dance. They would also study the ancient texts, astronomy, and the healing arts. It was considered a celebratory day, as the seventh day is the return to peace or oneness—the return to the One Law. The seventh day was the fulfilment of *shalama*, the Aramaic word for peace, which also means to be complete.

The seventh day is the culmination of the journey through the chakras, as we have arrived at the crown chakra. Traditionally often symbolised by a thousand-petalled lotus, this chakra is our connection to spirit, the Divine, or pure consciousness. The highest of the chakras pertaining to the physical body, the spinning vortex of the crown chakra emanates from the top of the head. At the crown chakra, we have the possibility of attaining unified consciousness. We are able to see the panoramic vista of life and how all is interconnected. This chakra helps us to listen to the "still, small voice within" and to the whisperings of our soul.

Humanity has believed, for scores of generations, that we are separate from other sentient beings upon the earth—that we are separate from all the other creatures and plants who inhabit the earth. We have believed this illusion is our reality because we became disconnected from nature and the earth, not seeing our part within creation.

To the Essenes, the unifying principle of all life was the

Divine. If we can see the divinity within all of life, if we can recognise that everything and everyone has the same essence, then we have the potential to become unified. In their language of Aramaic, the word for the Divine was *Alaha*, which translates as sacred unity. This is when all is unified in peace, wholeness, and love. The ultimate goal of the Essene was to attain this sacred unity of peace and live in harmony with the One Law.

The sacred marriage

The journey to attain this sacred unity is threefold. The first is that which begins inside ourselves—our inner unity and the unifying of our male and female energies within ourselves. The second level of unity is between our inner world and our outer world, between ourselves and nature. The third level of unity is with the whole of creation.

The first level of unity happens as a result of the transformational work we do with the angels. As our chakras are purified and balanced, the male and female energies within ourselves are united. This is called the inner marriage.

The inner marriage happens within each of us because each female contains both feminine energy and also masculine energy. Each male contains masculine energy and also feminine energy.

This is something that was known of by many ancient traditions. In terms of the energetics of our body, we are not purely all masculine or all feminine. The left side of our body is considered to have more of the feminine energies, the right side of our body more of the masculine energies. Whether we are a man or a woman, we always have within us the energies of both.

There is a continuous dance between the masculine and feminine energies within ourselves. As we journey with the angels and begin to love and accept ourselves more, this greater self-love leads to an awakening within ourselves. There is a stirring of the masculine and feminine energy currents that lie at the base of the spine. In the yogic tradition, these are known as Ida, the feminine energy current, and Pingala, the masculine energy current.

The seven chakras are located along the length of the spine, from the tip of the tailbone to the top of the head. Along the length of the spinal column and extending up towards the head, we also have a central channel called Susumna. This is the central axis for the flow of life force within our body, from our root to the top of our head.

With the energy of awakening, the feminine current, Ida, flows away from the central channel of Susumna to the left side, and Pingala, the masculine energy current, flows to the right side. They then arc back toward the central channel of Susumna, uniting at the sacral chakra in the belly.

The two energy currents, Ida and Pingala, then continue in their upward journey, arcing away from Susumna to then come together again at the next chakra, the solar plexus. Ida and Pingala continue to rise, unifying the masculine and feminine energies within each of the chakras, until they come to the brow chakra.

The brow is where the sacred inner marriage may take place, the ultimate union of the masculine and feminine energies within the self. The united masculine and feminine energies then ascend together to the crown chakra opening the thousand-petalled lotus—our doorway to unification with a greater consciousness.

The spiritual initiates of the Essenes were familiar with these practises. They have been kept alive in the yogic and tantric traditions of the east. As we harmonise our masculine and feminine energies within ourselves, we grow in our qualities of love and power, compassion and wisdom, and strength and vulnerability. These are an expression of our own wholeness as we "marry" our own inner male and female energies within. This is the first level of sacred unity.

The second level of unity is between ourselves and nature. This is a union between our inner nature and nature in the world around us. This is where we come to a point of knowing and feeling that we are a reflection of the living book of nature. We are one and the same as nature, because we breathe the same air as does the Mother Earth and all of her angels. We are one with the water that flows around the planet, and the sun that shines in the sky. We are one with the Mother Earth. A mission of the angels is to open our eyes to our oneness with Mother Nature. The world of nature around us does not change, but it is our relationship with Nature that will change.

The third level of unity is with all of life, with the whole of creation, with the Divine above and the earth below. This is the sacred unity of oneness with Alaha—the mystery of mysteries, the holy grail of the Essenes. The whole of existence is one of reflections, those within and without, above and below. It is a sacred dance of masculine and feminine energies.

To the mystical eye, the earth may be seen as a grail, a chalice of light containing all the beauty of creation. In the ancient Essene teachings, they spoke of the earth as a bride and the sun as a bridegroom, and each night as the sun descended, the mystical marriage took place. The earth is a feminine grail who waits to receive the light of the sun each dawn. This is the mystical marriage of male and female on a vast cosmic scale—a daily consummation creating life and love on the planet.

The Essenes revered the sun as the dwelling place of the angels. As colourful light beings, the angels are a bridge between the earth and the sun. They travel on the sacred breath, being in many places at one time. Our measure of time is not their reality, as they live in the eternal moment of *now*.

Peace with the divine is the ultimate transmutation of the self. This is not only a transformation of our thinking and our feeling, it is an alchemical change and purification of being; it is a change in our cells—a change in the very essence of who we are. We will see, once again, the golden threads that connect us to all beings. The world of the angels and the devas will become second nature to us. We have turned the golden key and glimpsed the realm of the angel of eternal life.

On the journey we may have many transitions of being; many changes may take place within us. As we come closer to the essence of our true self, we may find that our world may change— our relationships, work, or home. The walls of our ivory towers may crumble, as the nature of life is change. Healing ourselves will create change. The angels guide us to let go of the old and embrace the new, with a positive and optimistic heart.

Nature teaches us nothing stays static or still. The water is always moving, the breath is always flowing, and the clouds constantly change in the sky. Our Mother Earth is transforming our world. We live in a time of transition, and the Essenes believed it was the earth who would be the catalyst for change. The call for justice, fairness, equality, and unity has been heard. To live in unity is to honour each and every sentient being who lives upon the planet, whether seen or unseen, known or unknown.

The angel of eternal life

The angel of eternal life is an angel of the Divine who is closely associated with the earth. This angel has been here since the beginning of time and views from the angels' eyrie the unfolding changes occurring on Mother Earth. He is privy to the grand plan of creation and observes the smallest details. He is an angelic alchemist who waves his magic wand of healing and transformation.

With this angel's guidance, we become both loving and practical, kind and compassionate. These qualities grow as we put our roots down deep into the Mother Earth. Our roots need to be deep, for then we are able to hold onto the wings of the angel of eternal life and fly—to become the divine being we are destined to be, sacred in our own essence. The angel of eternal life oversees the birth of the new consciousness and ushers in the new earth.

The angel of eternal life is associated with the highest angels of the Divine, who are known as the architects of creation. These are huge angels, who turn the wheels of time and whose fingerprints are on every leaf and blade of grass. Their secrets were given to the angel of eternal life, and one of them is the mystery of the Tree of Life.

The knowledge of the Tree of Life was a mystical secret of the Essenes. Only the initiate who had worked with their inner process of transformation for seven years were given the secret knowledge of the Tree of Life.

The Tree of Life is a spiritual tree, which exists in an angel paradise. It contains all of the sacred knowledge about creation. The Essene Tree of Life is a tree that is comprised of angels, as each branch and each root is an angel. There are fourteen angels in all, as the seven roots are angels, and the seven branches are angels. Our ultimate spiritual destiny is to become one with the angels and the Tree of Life. It is to sit at the centre of the tree surrounded by the angels, with our roots deep within the Mother Earth and our soul ascending as the branches to touch the Divine. This is our return from whence we have come, before time was even measured. To become one with the Tree of Life and the angels is the spiritual unification of our soul with all.

The angels are our guides on our return journey to the Tree of Life and the garden of our soul. They are the light that draws us forward. They illuminate our path as a light that never dims and as a candle in the wind that is never extinguished.

In the Essene words:

I enter the eternal and infinite garden of mystery,
my spirit in oneness with the Divine, my body in
oneness with the Mother Earth, and my heart in

harmony with my Brothers. (*The Essene Gospel of Peace*)

Divine pattern and order

> The One Law fashioned the stars, the sun, the
> light and the darkness, and the sacred Law within
> our souls.
> —*The Essene Gospel of Peace*

The Essene wisdom harks back to the teachings of Enoch, he who became perfected man and who then became the archangel Metatron. Enoch lived millennia before the Essenes, and his teachings gave them their understanding of the One Law and also their calendars.

The archangel Metatron is the highest of all of the angels of the Divine. He contains the very essence of creation within his being. The secrets of the sacred pattern and order within creation are his domain, his influence encompassing both the heavens and the earth.

The love of this angel is all seeing and all knowing, and we are held in the crucible of his love as we live our daily lives. The love of the archangel Metatron is expressed in the smallest minutiae of life and the largest of the planets. Even the earth herself is but one planet embraced within this angel's love.

The Essenes believed in divine pattern and order as an expression of the One Law. The law of divine pattern and order is contained within a sacred pattern known as the *flower of life*. All of the patterns and cycles of creation are contained within this sacred symbol, as all of life is woven upon its perfect symmetry and form. The flower of life symbolises unity and the perfection of creation. Some believe in an accidental creation, but the Essenes believed everything was intricately crafted by the hand of the Divine.

The flower of life

The flower of life is a geometrical shape comprised of nineteen overlapping circles, arranged in a petal-like formation. The circles overlap, creating a symmetrical, hexagonal pattern. Philosophers from many ancient cultures have revered the flower of life as a sacred pattern. It's found in temples of many ancient cultures, such as those of Egypt, China, Japan, and Turkey.

The hand of the archangel Metatron is visible in all the minutiae of life, even the subatomic building blocks of life. The flower of life contains within it the *fruit of life*, which is considered to be the template for every single atom. And out of the fruit of life is born a primary structure of creation, known as Metatron's Cube.

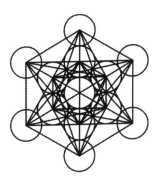

The fruit of life with Metatron's Cube

The fruit of life is comprised of thirteen circles; thirteen is a feminine number, and the circle a feminine symbol, whilst a straight line is a masculine symbol. If we connect each circle of the fruit of life to the centre of each other circle via a straight line, we create a geometric structure known as Metatron's Cube. In its creation there are the thirteen circles of the fruit of life connected by seventy-eight straight lines.

If we take the patterns of sacred geometry one step further, we come to the platonic solids. The geometrical shape of Metatron's Cube contains within itself the five platonic solids. These are the three-dimensional structures known as the tetrahedron, star tetrahedron, octahedron, dodecahedron, and icosahedron.

These are the five platonic solids that are the primary blueprints for all organic life. They are the building blocks of every seed, snowflake, mineral, shell, and even our DNA. Each of these, and all of life, is a manifestation of a cosmic blueprint of divine beauty and harmony. All is perfect pattern and order and an expression of the love of the Divine.

Sacred number, pattern, and form were well understood by the Essenes. Even the annual calendar they lived by was a part of this pattern and order, as their annual solar calendar was also given to them by Enoch and, so, was also intimately connected with the archangel Metatron.

The calendar was aligned with the same geometrical numbers that create Metatron's Cube—the numbers *thirteen* and *seventy-eight* (the thirteen circles and seventy-eight straight lines). Their calendar was comprised of four seasons of exactly thirteen weeks each, making a total of 91 days per season, which is again thirteen plus seventy-eight. The total number of days in their year was 364, which if we add the individual digits together comes to thirteen. Both Metatron's Cube and the Essene solar calendar, given to them by their great forefather Enoch, display the same numerical pattern—13/78/91.

The Essenes were masters in their understanding of the divine order, which was found in all life around them, and they aspired to live in unity with this order. Their feast days and their sabbath always followed the same annual and weekly pattern. Life to the Essenes was one of reverence to the Divine, but it was always a joyful expression of this, as they believed they lived in a paradise on earth.

The angel of eternal life opens our eyes to the divine love, to divine pattern and order that is expressed in all life around us, and to the extraordinary contained within the ordinary. The cycles of the sun and the moon, the seasons, the way leaves spiral around a flower's stem—with this angel, we may see the world as divine love expressed in many and diverse forms:

> The falling of leaves, the flow of rivers, the music
> of the insects at night, all these are ruled by the
> Law. (*The Essene Gospel of Peace*)

The return

We commence the seven-day cycle of angels with the angel of life, whose gift to us is peace with our body. We complete the cycle on the seventh day with the angel of eternal life, who gives us peace with the Divine and our own divinity. Life becomes eternal life as we embrace our divinity and unify with our soul. We become a divine microcosm within a divine macrocosm. The gift we have to offer in return is our service to the world; as we become peace, we can share that peace with others.

We will journey long and far, even before we lay hold of the wings of the angel of eternal life. But when we do, our angel chariot will carry us to our spiritual home, the eternal Tree of Life. There we will live as one with all of the angels, the Mother Earth, and the Divine.

Chapter 11

The Angels Are with Us

Live first in peace with all the angels, for then
your peace will be as a fountain that replenishes
itself with the giving.

—*The Essene Gospel of Peace*

If we wish to make a difference and create peace in our world,
then we need look no further than the teachings of the Essenes.
Theirs is an all-embracing and all-encompassing teaching, which
has also been proven through time. The Essenes were masters of
peace and consummate healers. They created a paradise in the
desert and sowed a seed of peace with the angels—a seed that is
ready to germinate now.

We can build on the energy of peace, which they sowed
with the angels. We can create a rainbow of peace, which ripples
through time zones, a planetary wave of peace. One can affect
many, and we learn from the angels that our thoughts fly free to
affect all. It follows that our thoughts of peace will affect all others
too. We may meditate with the angels in solitary comfort and still
be part of creating peace in our world.

We may be individuals in diverse locations, but we can
all make a difference to the energy of peace. Many individual
rainbows of light will create one giant rainbow that spans the
world. Our dream and the angels' dream are one dream—the
promise of the rainbow bridge of peace in the world.

Our dream of peace begins in our minds, is felt in our hearts,
and manifests in our actions. We can breathe the peace of the

angels, as we all share the one breath of spirit. As we breathe peace, we create the unity of peace.

The Essenes taught that only those who were at peace with the angels could share that peace with others. The angels are loving witnesses to our journey to become the angel that we are. Then we may fulfil the promise of the rainbow and be the peace we wish to see in the world—the peace that is sevenfold.

> To think the thoughts of the angels, to speak the words of the angels, and to do as the angels do.
>
> —*The Essene Gospel of Peace*

Chapter 12

The Angel Peace Meditation

We worship the sacred breath which is placed
higher than all other things created.
—*The Essene Gospel of Peace*

We have learned about the angels in our minds, and we have
felt their teachings in our hearts. Now we may learn how to bring
the two together in our actions. The action we may practise is to
meditate with the angels of peace, to invite them into our lives.
This is how we may create peace and how we may manifest the
seven gifts of peace from the angels.

There is a specific meditation we may use; and as in all things
Essene, it is borrowed from nature. The meditation is based on the
sky and the sun—a clear, radiant, pale blue sky and a brilliantly,
shining sun. The sky belongs to the angel of air and the breath.
The sun is the domain of the angel of the sun, who is love.

To meditate, we simply sit and imagine ourselves surrounded
by a large, pale blue bubble, which extends above our head and
beneath our feet. This is the same colour blue as the sky without
any clouds. The pale blue sky represents the perfectly peaceful
mind, as blue is the colour and the energy of peace. Beyond the
clouds of thought, there is always the blue sky of a peaceful mind.

At the centre of our body, just above the navel and a little
way inside, we imagine there is a brightly shining light, like an
internal sun, which fills our body with light from the inside.

This is a very simple and effective meditation, which takes little concentration once we are familiar with the visualisation.

The Essenes practised this meditation in the middle of the day, when the sun shone most brightly in the sky. This is not necessarily a practical time for some people, but if it is, then it is the perfect time. However, we need to be realistic about what is possible for us and remember the angels are present every minute of every day. Their healing powers are always available, and if it is easier to meditate in the morning or the evening, then that is the time for you. Trust the angels, and peace will follow.

Before you settle to meditate, ensure the words of the angel invocation of the day are in front of you. When you are settled and ready to meditate, say to yourself the words of the invocation to the angel. Close your eyes, relax, and enter the meditation. In the beginning, you may need to read the words of the invocations, but after awhile, you will come to know the angels and will no longer need the words.

As we enter the meditation, we focus on our breath as it gently flows in and out of our body. The breath is our connection with spirit. As to the Essenes, their word for breath was *Ruha*, which was also their word for spirit. As we breathe, we connect with our spirit and also the spirit of the angels. We breathe our way to peace. If we can spend twenty minutes of each day with the angels, we will transform our life and transform our world.

The Meditation

It is a good idea to take a few moments to settle before the meditation and make ourselves comfortable wherever we choose, either sitting on a chair or on the ground. If we are able to sit outside in nature, this is ideal but not necessary.

Open the book at the page of the day of the week.

We begin the meditation by reading the words of the invocation to the angel of the day.

This invites the presence of the angels of peace.

Relax and close the eyes.

Be present with the breath, as it gently flows in and out of the body.

Imagine you are sitting in a large pale blue bubble, the same colour as the sky without any clouds.

Imagine a brightly shining sun inside you. Just above the navel and a little way inside the body.

Relax with the visualisation.

Relax with the energy of the angels and the energy of peace.

Now we meditate with the angels and the visualisation for several minutes.

Be present with the breath as it gently flows into and out of the body.

Enjoy the feeling of peace.

Conclude gently at the end of the meditation, and on an out breath, open your eyes to a new moment, in your own time.

Chapter 13

Seven Angels in Seven Days

This chapter has been created for our ease of reference and is ideal to refer to as we practise the angel meditations. At the beginning of the chapter, we have each of the seven angel meditations available one page at a time. Each page includes the words of the angel invocations and their gifts of peace, as well as the day, chakra, and colour associations.

At the conclusion of this chapter is a chart, which has the seven angels and the seven days all visible on one page. This seven-day reference chart has been created with the first day of the week, Sunday, at the foot of the chart, and the seventh day of the week, Saturday, at the top. This is to keep the relationship between the days and the angels in their correct alignment with the chakras and the colours of the rainbow. The root chakra, day one, is at the bottom of the chart, and the crown chakra, day seven, is at the top.

Day One
Sunday
Angel of Life

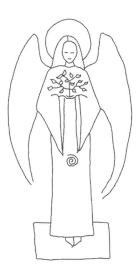

Angel invocation

I ask the Angel of Peace to always be with me,
and I ask the Angel of Life to bring health and
vitality to my body.

—The Essene Gospel of Peace

The gift of the angel of life is peace with the body

Root chakra: Red

Day Two
Monday
Angel of Power

Angel invocation

I ask the Angel of Peace to always be with me,
and I ask the Angel of Power to help me feel more
peaceful in my thoughts.

—The Essene Gospel of Peace

The gift of the angel of power is peace with the mind

Sacral chakra: Orange

Day Three
Tuesday
Angel of Love

Angel invocation

I ask the Angel of Peace to always be with me,
and I ask the Angel of Love to bring peace and
harmony to my family."

—*The Essene Gospel of Peace*

The gift of the angel of love is peace with the family

Solar plexus chakra: Yellow

Day Four
Wednesday
Angel of Creative Work

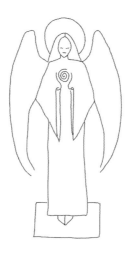

Angel invocation

I ask the Angel of Peace to always be with me, and I ask the Angel of Creative Work to be with all of humankind, that we may receive the blessing of our sacred task.

—*The Essene Gospel of Peace*

The gift of the angel of creative work is peace with humanity

Heart chakra: Green

Day Five
Thursday
Angel of Wisdom

Angel invocation

I ask the Angel of Peace to always be with me,
and I ask the Angel of Wisdom to guide my
knowledge, that I may walk in the paths of the
great ones who have seen the face of the Divine.
—*The Essene Gospel of Peace.*

The gift of the angel of wisdom is peace with culture

Throat chakra: Blue

Day Six
Friday
Angel of Joy

Angel invocation

I ask the Angel of Peace to always be with me, and I ask the Angel of Joy to be present upon the Mother Earth, that our hearts may be full of singing and gladness as we nestle in the arms of our Mother.

—*The Essene Gospel of Peace*

The gift of the angel of joy is peace with the Mother Earth

Brow chakra: Royal blue

Day Seven
Saturday
Angel of Eternal Life

Angel invocation

I ask the Angel of Peace to always be with me,
and I invoke the Angel of Eternal Life, that I may
soar beyond the stars and live forever.

—The Essene Gospel of Peace

The gift of the angel of eternal life
is peace with the Divine

Crown chakra: Violet

	DAY	ANGEL	PEACE WITH	CHAKRA	COLOUR
7	Saturday	Angel of Eternal Life	The Divine	Crown	Violet
6	Friday	Angel of Joy	Mother Earth	Brow	Royal Blue
5	Thursday	Angel of Wisdom	Culture	Throat	Sapphire Blue
4	Wednesday	Angel of Creative Work	Humanity	Heart	Green
3	Tuesday	Angel of Love	Family	Solar Plexus	Yellow
2	Monday	Angel of Power	Mind	Sacral	Orange
1	Sunday	Angel of Life	Body	Root	Red

Seven Angels, Seven Days

Bibliography

Booth, Mike, *Aura-Soma Handbook*, UK, John Michael Booth, 2000.

Flavius, Josephus, *The Essene Code of Life*, trans., Edmond Bordeaux Szekely, USA, International Biogenic Society, 1978.

Szekely, Edmond Bordeaux, trans., *The Essene Gospel of Peace*, USA, Academy Books, 1974.

Vermes, Geza, *The Complete Dead Sea Scrolls in English*, UK, Penguin Books, 2004.

Notes

Printed in the United States
By Bookmasters